W9-ARC-278

3 9077 03941748 3

623.86 Koza, Thad
KOZ

The tall ships

9/97

DISCARD

08/16

FAIRPORT PUBLIC LIBRARY
1 Village Landing
Fairport, NY 14450

Published by Tide-mark Press Ltd.
P.O. Box 280311, East Hartford, CT 06128-0311

Distributed in Canada by Monarch Books of Canada

Distributed in the U.K. by Lavis Marketing.

Printed in Singapore by Craft Print

Design and typography by Jane Kirk

Special thanks to Lorraine Alexson and Robert Manning for their work on this manuscript.

Copyright 1996 by Thaddeus Koza and Tide-mark Press

All rights reserved.
No part of this book may be reproduced in any form or by any electronic or mechanical means
without written permission from the publisher; reviewers, however, may quote brief passages in the context of a review.

First printing

Library of Congress Catalog Number 96-61174

ISBN 1-55949-313-5

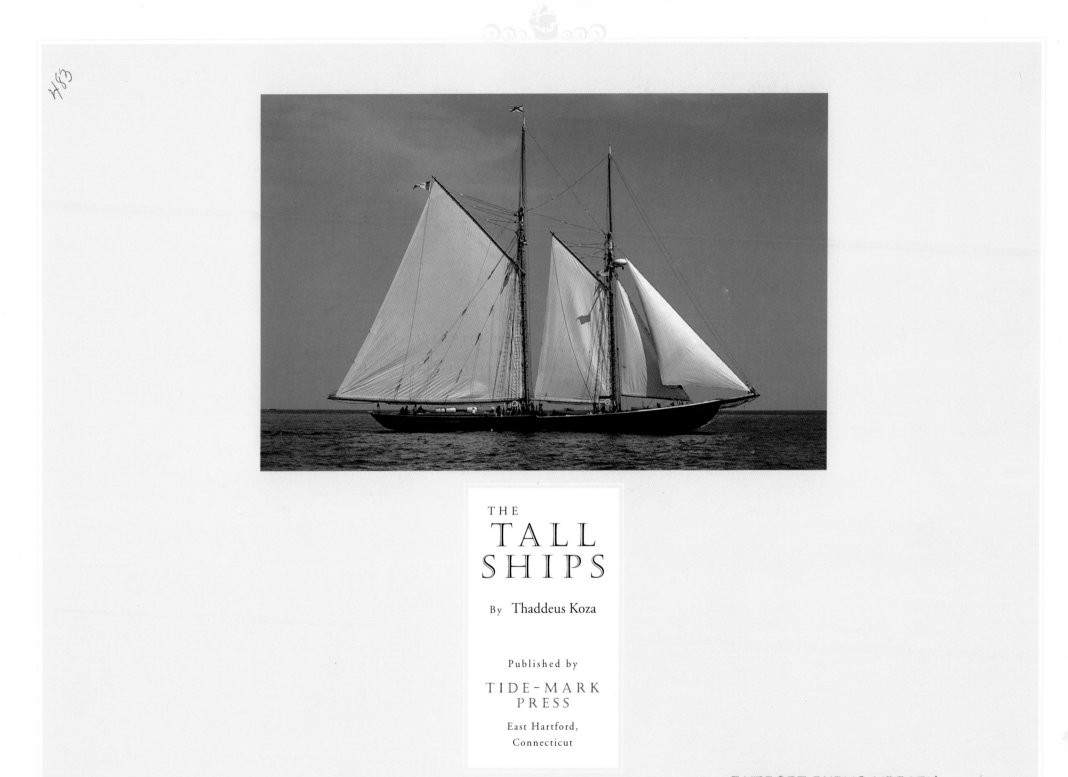

THE
TALL
SHIPS

By Thaddeus Koza

Published by

TIDE-MARK PRESS

East Hartford,
Connecticut

FAIRPORT PUBLIC LIBRARY
1 VILLAGE LANDING
FAIRPORT, N.Y. 14450

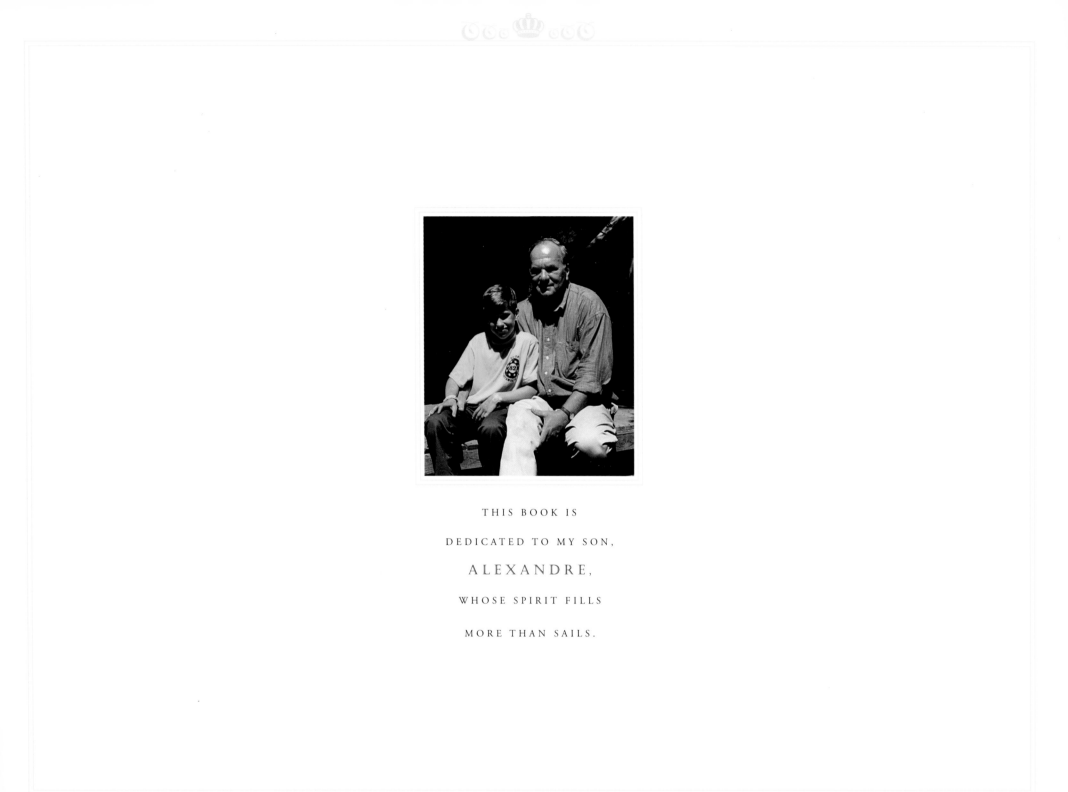

THIS BOOK IS

DEDICATED TO MY SON,

ALEXANDRE,

WHOSE SPIRIT FILLS

MORE THAN SAILS.

CONTENTS

ACKNOWLEDGMENTS

Jay Babina of Jason Designs, Branford, CT.

Susan Berman and her staff at the North Kingstown, Rhode Island Public Library who have discovered the facts on the "flotsam and jetsam" of my mind's wanderings.

Zygmunt Choren, *Choren Designs*, Gdansk, Poland.

Ole R. Iversen, Sec.-Gen., *Stifelsen Skoleskipet Christian Radich*, Oslo, Norway.

Robin Krohn of the Maritime and Seafood Industry Museum of Biloxi, Mississippi.

Per Langhelle, General Manager, *Stiftelsen Seilskipet Statsraad Lehmkuhl*, Bergen, Norway.

Peter Smales of the Cutty Sark Press Office, London.

Jeff Szala, *Museum of Yachting*, Newport, Rhode Island.

Mrs. Esther Tibbs, Marketing Officer, Sail Training Association (STA), Hampshire, United Kingdom.

Pamela Wuerth and Martha Provost of the American Sail Training Association in Newport, Rhode Island.

There are a number of captains and masters who have lent their time and deck space, knowledge and hospitality to assist in the pursuit of this project. Among the many are: Captain Joe Davis, Capt. Emilio de Rogatis, Capt. Kip Files, Capt. Pete Hall, Capt. Jan Miles, Capt. Tadeusz Olechnowicz, Capt. Dan Quinn, Capt. Rob Rustchak, Capt. Henryk Sniegocki, and Capt. Witek Zdrojewski.

And finally, to the FAB FIVE of Ann Arbor:
Bob, Fred, Jay, Paul, and Ross who have provided snug harbors and sound advice for as long as the rhumb line of this passage to print has taken, and then some.

Photographs
The author wishes to acknowledge several photographers who contributed their work to this book:

Toshi Yamazaki for the photograph of *Akogare*,

Inland Seas Education Association for *Inland Seas*,

Azuma Yasuo for *Nippon Maru II*, and

Gary Pearl for *Victory Chimes*.

TALL SHIPS IN THE 20TH CENTURY

Is there a place for 19th century sailing ships in the 20th century? Is there a reason and a way to save great sailing ships from extinction despite evolving technology which seems to sound their inevitable death knell? Those are questions a group of sailing enthusiasts began asking in England during the 1950s. They formed the Sail Training Association (STA) and started what has become an international movement that promises to make a place for tall ships in the coming century.

In 1973 the American Sail Training Association (ASTA) was formed as an affiliate of STA by Barclay Warburton, owner of the brigantine *Black Pearl.* Today, ASTA is one of many national sail training associations around the world which have grown out of STA. Aided by ASTA in the United States, and related groups around the world, many large sailing vessels have confounded technological evolution and adopted important new roles.

In the United States and Canada, there are many sail training vessels which serve as laboratories and classrooms at sea. College and high school students regularly embark on semester-long voyages of offshore discovery while younger children explore local waters on grade-school field trips. Water, sediment, and biological sampling provide students with tangible lessons in the marine environment as they physically encounter the effect of wind and wave. Formal study aboard a ship is frequently referred to as sea education.

Historic vessels, or their reproductions, function as interpretive museum exhibits, conducting voyages of outreach to the public. Most North Americans can trace their ancestors' arrival by ship. The last sailing vessel to regularly carry immigrants to America still plies New England waters, now a sailing school vessel, extending her venerable history of more than one hundred years service — from fishing the Grand Banks to Arctic exploration to African packet.

There are reproductions and restorations of ships representative of each of America's naval conflicts. We may board important sailing ships of the American Revolution, the War of 1812, the Civil War, and some which played their part in the World Wars. We may experience life at sea aboard Grand Banks fishing schooners, mackerel seiners, oyster boats, and whalers. Cargo ships. Pilot boats. Merchant vessels. Immigrant ships. Those pressed into the slave trade. There is not a chapter of our history which does not have a waterborne link. The smell of pine tar and manila, the sounds of a working ship, the sighting of a whale on the horizon from the top of the rig, the motion of a rolling deck — history is a compelling study in this physical context.

Other North American ships sail ambassadorial missions for the public they serve, issuing invitations of hospitality and promoting opportunities for economic development. Other ships sail to save the environment or to promote international relations through citizen diplomacy, as did a Soviet-American crew sailing past the final sputters of the Cold War. These vessels draw our attention and focus us on their missions because sailing ships are powerful icons symbolizing strength, beauty, and harmony wherever they go. Those who sail recognize the ocean as a link which connects us to foreign lands — not a boundary which separates us.

Several American sail training ships serve as residential treatment centers for adjudicated youth while others provide exclusive corporate team building exercise or offshore adventure travel — from coastal cruising with gourmet cooking to blue water voyaging. While the clientele could not be more different, these ships are all in the business of enrichment.

As diverse an agenda as this may seem at first glance, these ships all provide sail training. The common denominator is that each uses wind and sea to teach us something. Sail training, like reading, is not a subject in and of itself. It is a means to an end. A medium. An environment. We at ASTA often say that sail training is not learning to sail, it is learning from sailing. From the ship, from the sea, and perhaps most importantly, from yourself.

A ship at sea has been described as a microcosm of the planet. Resources are finite, waste must be managed responsibly, and success depends on one's ability to work as a team. One quickly learns that many hands lighten a load. In a similar way, so do good shipmates — those who are focused, considerate, and good humored. There is no place on earth which better illuminates leadership qualities, nor marks the path so clearly toward achieving them. The rewards of a smoothly run ship are immediate, obvious, and sweetly satisfying. As sailors have said for centuries, take care of your ship and she'll take care of you.

There is no better feeling in the world than coming off an early morning watch having seen the sun rise and helped to scrub everything down for the start of a new day. As you leave the ship in the hands of the next watch you realize how happy you are to see them — and even happier to leave them to it — as you go below for the sort of breakfast you'd never eat ashore and a grateful climb into a narrow berth assuming any angle of heel. Adjusting to sleeping when you can is strangely easy, and you find yourself sleeping easily in your bunk no matter the time of day or the weather (well, with the occasional notable exception!). You find yourself frequently aware of living completely in the moment, and you take great pride in accomplishing tasks and seeking new challenges for yourself.

Aboard a sail training vessel, as in life, our small piece is a critical part of the whole. The quality of our work, and the spirit in which we do it, has a profound effect on the well-being of everyone else aboard. Leadership, paradoxically, is arrived at by learning to take direction. Becoming a team player. Pulling your share of the load. Being absolutely responsible. Dependable. And, learning to depend on the responsibility of others. For no matter what the particular mission of a ship might be, it is essential that she be safely navigated and handsomely attended.

This is true of the larger world, but in that larger world, the quality of our actions are not so immediately apparent. In our day-to-day lives, most of us do not have at hand accessible evidence of collisions we've safely avoided, environmental conditions we gained advantage from, or courses accurately steered no matter the conditions. Our actions seem at times to be in a vacuum and feedback is often clouded by other issues. It often takes years to measure the efficacy of our navigation and our ability to "hand, reef and steer" our lives. Nor do we often have the simple yet somehow completely thrilling affirmation of perfectly set sails in a stiff breeze and a ship "with a bone in her teeth." On a sail training vessel, it is right there. Right now.

For some, sail training offers first time successes. For others, it is a much needed refresher course in life when we find ourselves, for instance, knocking hats off passersby or staring too long at funeral processions — which Herman Melville describes as "high time to get to sea" in *Moby Dick*. For all, sail training offers an absolutely unique learning experience.

So, no, we don't just teach sailing. The ships illustrated in this book foster opportunities for intensive personal development — intensive life experience in order to advance leadership development, an utter reverence for nature, a sense of time and place, an appreciation for history, and teamwork ability. Sail training really teaches the qualities of stewardship, resourcefulness, pride, humility, bravery, strength, and grace. And we learn to sail, too.

Pamela C. Wuerth
Executive Director
August 1996

TALL SHIP RIGS

FULL-RIGGED SHIP
Three or more masts, all square-rigged

BARQUE
Three or more masts, all square-rigged except the aftermast which is fore-and-aft rigged

BRIG
Two masts, both square-rigged

BARQUENTINE
Three or more masts, all fore-and-aft rigged except the foremast which is fully square-rigged

BRIGANTINE
Two masts, the foremast is fully square-rigged and the mainmast is fore-and-aft rigged

TOPSAIL SCHOONER
Two or more masts, the foremast carries square-rigged sails over fore-and-aft sails

SCHOONER
Two or more masts, fore-and-aft rigged

THE RIG AND SAIL PLAN OF STATSRAAD LEHMKUHL

Norway's largest and oldest sailing ship, *Statsraad Lehmkuhl* has a displacement of 1701 gross tons. She has a sail area of 2026 square meters (21,800 square feet) distributed among 22 sails. The addition of modern accommodations reduced the ship's capacity for trainees from 200 to 150. There are cabins for the regular crew of 20. An 1125 h.p. diesel engine is capable of moving the ship at up to 11 knots in fair weather.

In consideration of the cadets' security, *Statsraad Lehmkuhl* was originally given a reduced rig relative to its size. This is a handicap when racing with other Class A vessels in light wind, however, the ship sails well in more robust conditions.

The accompanying illustrations is provided through the courtesy of Stiftelsen Seilskipet Statsraad Lehmkuhl, Holmedalsgården, Bryggen, N5003, Bergen, Norway.

SAILS

1 Flying jib
2 Outer jib
3 Inner jib
4 Fore topmast staysail
5 Fore course sail
6 Fore lower topsail
7 Fore upper topsail
8 Fore topgallant sail
9 Fore royal
10 Main royal staysail
11 Main topgallant staysail
12 Main topmast staysail
13 Main course sail
14 Main lower topsail
15 Main upper topsail
16 Main topgallant sail
17 Main royal
18 Mizzen topgallant staysail
19 Mizzen topmast staysail
20 Mizzen staysail
21 Mizzen
22 Mizzen gaff-topsail

MASTS AND YARDS

23 Bowsprit
24 Fore Mast
25 Fore Yard
26 Fore Lower cross-trees
27 Fore Lower topsail yard
28 Fore topmast
29 Fore upper topsail yard
30 Fore topmast cross-trees
31 Fore topgallant mast
32 Fore topgallant yard
33 Fore royal mast
34 Fore royal yard
35 Fore masthead
36 Main mast
37 Main yard
38 Main lower cross-trees
39 Main lower topsail yard
40 Main topmast
41 Main upper topsail yard
42 Main topmast cross-trees
43 Main topgallant mast
44 Main topgallant yard
45 Main royal mast
46 Main royal yard
47 Main masthead
48 Spanker boom
49 Mizzenmast
50 Spanker gaff
51 Mizzen cross-trees
52 Mizzen topmast
53 Mizzen topgallant mast
54 Mizzen masthead

CLASSES OF TALL SHIPS

As tall ships travel around the world, they frequently race with one another from port to port. Since hull length is a major determinant of speed through the water, these vessels have been grouped into classes to keep the competition fair.

Class A includes all square-rigged vessels over 120 feet (36.6m) in length overall, as well as fore-and-aft rigged vessels of 160 feet (48.8m) or more in length overall.

Class A, Division II covers all square-rigged vessels (including ships, barques, barquentines, brigs, and brigantines) less than 120 feet (36.6m) in overall length.

Class B includes fore-and-aft rigged vessels (topsail schooners, schooners, ketches, yawls, cutters, and sloops) of between 160 feet (48.8m) and 120 feet (36.6m) long overall.

Class C covers all other fore-and-aft rigged vessels with a waterline length of at least 30 feet (9.14m) in three divisions. Division one covers all gaff-rigged vessels of less than 100 feet (30.5m) not racing with spinnakers and all vessels built before 1939 not already included in Classes A, AII, and B. Division two includes all Bermudian-rigged vessels of less than 100 feet overall not racing with spinnakers. Division three covers all vessels of less than 100 feet (30.5m) long overall racing with spinnakers.

Note that length overall is the length between the forward end of the stem post and the after end of the stern post. It does not include the bowsprit, pulpit or any other extension at the bow or stern.

Pictured here are three different classes of tall ships. The largest of the three is *Sagres II* (with white sails), a Class A. *Roseway* is a Class B and carries tanbark sails. The smallest vessel and a Class C is the Polish sloop *Smuga Ciena*.

Together, four of the largest tall ships in the world measure more than a quarter of a mile from stem to stern. They are (left to right) *Kruzenshtern* at 376 feet, *Esmeralda* at 371 feet, *Sedov* at 386 feet and *Libertad* at 356 feet.

TALL SHIPS, TALL SHIPS!

Whenever the call is sounded around the world–from major ports of commerce to obscure havens from bad weather–a vast cloud of sail on the horizon sparks the interest and imagination of people everywhere. Tall ships are living memories of another era. They bespeak the adventures of nautical exploration and trade and the dangers and rewards of war at a time when far-flung people and countries discovered one another by crossing the sea. Today, tall ships recall the classic sailing vessels of centuries past as well as the sophisticated vessels that preview the technology of the twenty-first century.

From wooden brigs and schooners to modern steel-hulled barques and ships, tall ships combine elegant form with necessary function. Some vessels recall the fiction of Joseph Conrad, C. S. Forester, and Patrick O'Brian, while others–like *Kruzenshtern, Gazela, Creoula,* and *Bluenose II*–harken back to the less romantic heritage of cargo and fishing vessels. Some tall ships, like the HMS *Bounty* and the *Providence,* personify historic periods and events; others–*Pacific Swift* and *Corwith Cramer,* for example–chart new frontiers in education and exploration.

Not all tall ships are alike, in form or in function, nor should all tall ships be referred to as ships, at least so far as the formal nautical term is applied. Although we often use the term *ship* to characterize any large, sea-going vessel, it has a precise technical definition that refers to a ship's sail plan. The differences between tall ships, loosely defined, are seen in their sizes and hull designs and most especially in their rigging and sails, which reflect the ship's function and where in the ocean (on- or offshore, for example) the ship operates.

The Old English word *scip* gave us the word *ship* and generally refers to sea-going vessels as opposed to boats, which are generally smaller, open, and work in coastal areas. More formally, a full-rigged ship is a vessel with at least three masts and a bowsprit, which carries square sails on every mast. (For examples, see the entries for *Georg Stage* and *Sørlandet.*) The "modern" ship was designed in 1585 by Sir John Hawkins. Though ships grew larger over time, Hawkins's plan remained unchanged for the next three centuries. Built for the high seas, ships served as men-of-war and saw more traditional service as cargo vessels, which, in the nineteenth century, achieved their highest levels of speed and performance as *clippers* or *packet boats.*

Despite its success, the sail plan of square-rigged ships imposes severe limitations on a ship's maneuverability. Because most square-riggers cannot come closer than 65° to 70° of the true wind direction, intricate tacking and wearing maneuvers—a precise evolution of sail handling and rudder direction—are required to work the ship to windward. Square-riggers reached their peak with the famous Donald McKay clipper ships sailing the trade-wind routes at the turn of the century.

Once the standard for full-rigged ships was established, variations on the theme continued, as they had throughout nautical history. For example, *barques,* originally smaller vessels, evolved into deep-water cargo vessels. Barques are sailing ships with three or more masts, with the aftermost mast, or mizzen, rigged with a fore-and-aft sail, topped with a gaff. The sail is often referred to as gaff-headed. In a barque with three masts, the aftermast is termed a mizzen. In a four-masted barque, the aftermast is a spanker. In a five masted barque the sails are designated: fore, main, mizzen, spanker and driver. (For examples, see the *Eagle, Simon Bolivar,* and *Cuauhtemoc* entries.) The international fleet's largest vessels are four-masted barques, such as the German-built *Kruzenshtern* and *Sedov,* which both now fly the Russian flag. The twin Japanese four-masted barques (*Kaiwo Maru II* and *Nippon Maru II*) are sail training vessels designed along the lines of a predecessor ship. Three-masted barques have been the choice of Colombia, Ecuador, Mexico, United States, and Venezuela. The *Eagle, Gorch Fock II, Tovarishch, Mircea,* and *Sagres II* are classic ships of their type.

Because they require fewer hands to set sail and can sail closer to the wind than square-riggers, vessels with gaff-rigged fore-and-aft sails are popular on modern sailing vessels from training ships to yachts. The rig takes its name from the gaff, a spar parallel to the boom, used to hoist the head of the four-sided sail. Gaff rig defines a sail configuration which is distinct from square-riggers or yachts with more typical Bermudian (triangular) sails.

Other types of vessels are variations of square-rigged ships. There are brigs (*Fryderyk Chopin* and *Astrid*), brigantines (*Swan fan Makkum* and *Søren Larsen*), and barquentines (*Concordia* and *Gazela*). A brig has two masts, and both carry square topsails as well as a gaff-headed mainsail and mizzensail. A brigantine is similar to a brig except that it lacks the large cross-jack sail on the mainmast. A barquentine carries three or more masts, but the foremast alone is square-rigged. The difference between the four-masted vessels *Juan Sebastian del Elcano* and the elegant *Esmeralda* is that the foremast of the former is rigged with square sails above the fore-and-aft gaff sail, designating her as a topsail schooner. *Esmeralda's* foremast is rigged only with square sails, designating her as a barquentine.

Vessels designed to navigate coastal waters and inlets or fish close to shore have shallow keels and sail plans that adjust to shifting winds and tides. Thus we have *schooners* and *skipjacks*. In fact, the variations of sail plans are extraordinarily diverse and reflect thousands of years of sailing history. Each ship's masts and sails create a distinctive silhouette that adds to the mystique and magic of watching a ship leave harbor on the evening tide.

Beyond the rigging, particular hull configurations and adaptations lead to a larger number of variations. Thus, by substituting moveable leeboards or centerboards for fixed keels, shallow-draft ketches, known as *ewers* in Europe and *oyster schooners* in the Americas, were adapted to the needs of their work.

Cadets on *Dar Mlodziezy*

SCHOOL SHIPS

As the range and complexity of ships and navigation increased, the value of formal sailing schools became apparent. School ships were organized in the nineteenth century when the principal maritime nations recognized a need to have well-trained crews for their navies as well as for their increasingly valuable merchant vessels. Northern European countries like Denmark, Germany, and Norway were among the earliest to commit to these essential programs.

The German word *Segelschulschiffe,* or sailing school ship, perhaps best conveys the concept that led to the prototype barques built during the 1930s at the Blohm & Voss shipyards in Hamburg, Germany, and which were later replicated in Japanese, Polish, and Spanish shipyards. These shipboard academies evolved throughout the twentieth century into a modern variation of "classrooms afloat" in vessels as divergent as the *Concordia, Fryderyk Chopin, Kaisei,* and the *Lord Nelson,* all of which were built in the past decade. Their curricula are now less often concerned with training young people for a life at sea than with combining the study of sailing and the building of character with academic subjects like oceanography and marine biology and ecology.

The largest and most elegant of the vessels, however, are still part of government-sponsored naval training programs that also serve as their country's goodwill ambassadors by participating in such international events as Sail 2000 and such major maritime festivals as Operation Sail and Sail Amsterdam. Those gatherings also provide opportunities for the crews of tall ships to reinforce common bonds through camaraderie, mutual respect, and discipline.

More tall ships have been built since 1976, with more divergent crews and programs than would ever have seemed possible fifty years ago. Tall ships were an endangered species in 1950s when the Sail Training Association (STA) was formed in England. What was then a fleet of a few dozen ships has grown into an international fleet of two hundred. That number is growing, along with a host of international and national associations.

Japan and Russia lead in the national support of tall ships, both in numbers and in the sizes of cadet training programs. In the late 1980s the Japanese Institute for Sea Training built its newest four-masted barques, *Kaiwo Maru II* and *Nippon Maru II,* while the Russians have tenaciously sustained their last pair of four-masted barques, built in an earlier age—*Kruzenshtern* and *Sedov.* Concurrently, independent programs for groups as small as families and as large as medium-sized American cities now support efforts to build or restore vessels to the international fleet.

As different as are the rigs of the ships themselves, these school programs vary in duration and focus, from the length of time they are at sea to the level of training cadets may reach. From day-long sails aboard the *Quinnipiack* to six-month voyages aboard the *Cuauhtemoc,* the ships deliver their precious cargoes–students, cadets, and their respective cultures–to the world. *Eagle* prepares cadets from the United States Coast Guard Academy; *Concordia* educates high school students during a nine-month course of study that generally includes a long-term voyage. Students of oceanography at a number of colleges and universities in the United States and Canada complete semesters-at-sea aboard the vessels *Corwith Cramer* and *Westward,* which operate out of Woods Hole, Massachusetts, and the Caribbean. Cadets aboard *Danmark* and *Amerigo Vespucci* prepare for service as officers in their national navies. Several of the newer fully rigged ships built for Soviet Russia are now part of its Ministry of Fisheries and train staff for that essential industry.

LIFE ON BOARD

Aside from a few private yachts that fall into the category of tall ships, most vessels structure time on board into watches for the crew and officers. The two most common schedules divide the day into three or four watches; that is, either six hours on, twelve hours off, and six hours on again or four hours on and eight hours off, and so on. For younger members of the crew, this schedule includes a formal curriculum of classes and study. Depending on the ship and the educational institution it represents, the curriculum might lead directly to licensure in the merchant marine service or give credit toward a college degree in the marine sciences or to the completion of a secondary-school course that is part of an affiliated high school system.

Once on board, sharing a cabin with one to nine other crew members (and occasionally there are squad bays or large open spaces where hammocks are still triced up in

Peeling and socializing on *Dar Mlodziezy*

the manner of a bygone era, a method still used on *Christian Radich*), cadets fall into a pattern of duties on deck that are part of sailing the ship, along with training sessions in navigation, course setting, and communications. Even mundane tasks, such as staffing the galley, are part of a crew's work. More than just work, however, joining a group for potato peeling is also an opportunity to socialize.

As sophisticated as the crew's course work may be, including satellite hookups to research centers, the most routine situations can serve to reintroduce a ship's traditional role. As the vessel *Tole Mour* underwent a U.S. Coast Guard safety inspection in Boston harbor a couple of years ago, a ship necessity was discovered missing: there was no cargo net. Officers used their knowledge of traditional marlinespike seamanship skills to hitch a cargo net from retired running rigging. The occasion became an opportunity to teach traditional skills and lore to new crew members while tapping the imaginative resources of the experienced mariners on board.

Hammocks triced up below decks on *Statsraad Lehmkuhl*

Ships develop their own distinctive cultures, and everything from the inevitable T-shirt to characteristic turkshead bracelets become part of the nautical experience. Visits to harbors are highlighted by "parades of sail" and by ceremonial processions of crews for host audiences.

Throughout a cruise, the long tradition of older, experienced hands passing on their knowledge and understanding to the young persists, whether that includes the "splicing of an eye," the skill to build ships in bottles, or "reading" the sea and sky to foresee the weather ahead.

A BROTHERHOOD
OF THE SEA

A decade after the end of World War II several sailing enthusiasts and historians realized that the old sailing vessels of the nineteenth and twentieth centuries were an endangered species, relics whose time and importance had been surpassed by newer technology, and particularly by the airplane.

A retired London attorney, Bernard Morgan, began promoting the "dream of a brotherhood of the sea" that would bring together the ships and youth of seafaring peoples into a friendly rivalry leavened with a common interest in sharing the best experiences of life at sea. With the encouragement of Comdr. Peter Godwin and Capt. John Illingworth, a committee, the International Sail Training Race Committee, was formed in the autumn of 1954. This committee, supported by the tireless efforts of Portuguese ambassador Pedro Theotonia Pereira, established the first organized tall ship race, which went from Torbay to Lisbon in 1956.

This race, between just seven vessels, signaled the start of a series of gatherings that introduced tall ships to generations of people for whom they had largely been forgotten. Two of the vessels that participated in that first race, *Mercator* and *Creole,* have recently been restored and are again among the ships making appearances at major tall ship events. The success of the original race led directly to the formation of the Sail Training Association, which began organizing small gatherings of sailing vessels every other year. STA has now developed into a parent organization that oversees at least one major event annually.

In 1964 the world's fair in New York was saluted by the appearance of a number of national sail training vessels. Their appearance promoted interest, enthusiasm, and support for an American organization like STA. Twelve years later, the American Sail Training Association (ASTA) was formed for the celebration of America's bicentennial in 1976. That event brought a fleet of more than two hundred vessels to New York for the 4th of July celebration and additional parades of sail in outlying ports. Those events led to the creation of a series of national and local organizations and committees. Operation Sail, Sail Boston, Sail Baltimore, and the Sausalito Tall Ships Society are some of the groups that have preserved vessels or created sailing and educational programs that sustain the ideals of STA and sail training in general.

Corresponding to the American developments of ASTA and the Canadian Sail Training Association (CSTA), European nations have followed suit and formed their own STA's, including: APORVELA (Portugal), STAF (Finland), STAG (Germany), STAJ (Japan),STAN (Netherlands), STAP (Poland), and STAR (Russia). To oversee the planning, policies, and scheduling of all these energetic groups, the umbrella group, the International Sail Training Association (ISTA), was formed, with representatives from all member STA's.

Under ISTA, municipal governments and private corporations around the world now develop plans and schedule events to bring tall ships together. In the United States, Gloucester Schooner Days, the Great Chesapeake Bay Schooner Race, Operation Sail, Sail Baltimore, Sail Boston, and Tall Ships Newport have generated interest in tall ships.

In turn, most ships have a home organization or affiliation that supports sailing programs. Whether a federation of programs such as the Sea Education Association (SEA) in Woods Hole, Massachusetts, which places students abroad, or a local foundation, such as the Living Classroom Foundation in Baltimore, Maryland, these administrations function as fund-raisers and suppliers of crews for the programs and passages of the vessels.

Hitching a net on *Tole Mour*

THE
TALL
SHIPS

AKOGARE

Built by the city of Osaka, Japan, as a good-will ambassador for the municipality, *Akogare* is the latest vessel to join the expanding Japanese sail training fleet. Her name means "the yearning," and she is a topsail schooner that began sailing and training programs in 1994. She will serve as the flagship for Sail Osaka '97, the international gathering of tall ships in Japan.

SCANTLINGS
Length overall: 171'
Beam: 28' 6"
Draft: 13'
Hull: Steel
Rig: Topsail schooner
Year built: 1993
Home port: Osaka, Japan
Flag: Japan

SCANTLINGS
Length overall: 205'
Beam: 26'
Draft: 15'6"
Hull: Steel
Rig: Barque
Year built: 1906; converted, 1986
Home port: Bremerhaven, Germany
Flag: Germany

ALEXANDER von HUMBOLDT

Outfitted in distinctive green sails, *Alexander von Humboldt* is the flagship of the Sail Training Association of Germany (STAG). Originally operated as the lightship *Kiel,* she maintained her position in the Baltic for eighty years. Retiring in 1986, she underwent extensive refitting and conversion under the supervision of Polish naval architect Zygmunt Choren.

Lightships occupy a fixed position at sea. They are outfitted with navigational lighting and sound devices to warn other ships of their position. Because of their strong hull construction, lightships are good candidates for conversion to sail. During that process the interior is rebuilt and running rigging and spars are added, along with auxiliary engines. (See also entries for *Atlantis, Den Store Bjørn,* and *Europa.*)

As the sail training vessel of STAG, *Alexander von Humboldt* now visits ports around the world as a goodwill ambassador, especially for young people with an interest in science.

The ship is named for the German scientist, traveler, and statesman Alexander von Humboldt,1769–1859, who was also the founder of Berlin University. Von Humboldt explored South America from 1799 to 1804. His interest in isothermal conditions and the weather led him to devise a systematic strategy for agricultural development. In honor of his contributions to the understanding of the ocean and its ecology, the South Pacific's Humboldt Current was named for him.

ALEXANDRIA

This three-masted topsail schooner represents the city of Alexandria, Virginia, at many of the maritime festivals on the Atlantic coast. She is 125 feet in overall length, is built of wood, and has the characteristic tanbark sails and lines of classic Baltic traders.

Originally the three-masted schooner *Ingve*, this vessel was extensively restored and re-rerigged in the Danish shipyard of J. Ring-Andersen in 1973 by Brian Watson. At that time she emerged as the topsail schooner *Lindø* and appeared at the U.S. bicentennial celebration in New York in 1976. After serving as a private vessel on the east coast, she was acquired by the Alexandria Seaport Foundation in 1986. She now serves as a representative for that city, as well as having an extensive program of sail training, maritime skills, and boat building for youth.

SCANTLINGS
Length overall: 125'
Beam: 22'
Draft: 9'
Hull: Wood
Rig: Topsail schooner
Year built: 1929
Home port: Alexandria, Virginia
Flag: United States

AMERICA

Presenting a striking profile with notably raked masts, this black-hulled schooner sustains the tradition of speed, elegance, and innovation established by her namesake. She is a re-creation of the most famous racing yacht in history, the schooner *America*, which won the 100-guinea cup, now known as *America's Cup*, in 1851. Constructed with the assistance of fifteen major marine product manufacturers, she was built from the waterline up to replicate the lines and design of the original. *America's* 139-foot wood-and-epoxy composite hull was completed in the fall of 1995 by Scarano Boat Building of Albany, New York.

Traveling throughout the world to demonstrate the best and most innovative products of the National Marine Manufacturing Association, *America* will sail the seven seas and maintain an aggressive travel schedule, averaging more than 20,000 miles annually.

SCANTLINGS
Length overall: 139'
Beam: 25'
Draft: 10'
Hull: Wood
Rig: Schooner
Year Built: 1995
Home port:
Alexandria, Virginia
Flag: United States

AMERICAN EAGLE

In 1984, after fifty-three years of hard fishing in the Atlantic, *American Eagle* underwent a major reconstruction at the North End Shipyard in Camden, Maine. Local stands of white pine, locust, and oak were used for her solid timber reconstruction. Thanks to the ingenuity and expertise of six schooner captains, *American Eagle* returned to the sea, joining the Maine schooner fleet.

She is now designated a national historic landmark. Her fair lines and tarred rigging bring back memories of her launch three generations ago. Today, with varnished interior cabins, an all-weather rig, and contemporary safety features, *American Eagle* is seaworthy, fast, and outfitted for comfort and convenience.

SCANTLINGS
Length overall: 121'
Beam: 20'
Draft: 11' 6"
Hull: Wood
Rig: Schooner
Year built: 1930
Home port: Rockland, Maine
Flag: United States

SCANTLINGS
Length overall: 135'
Beam: 24'
Draft: 9'
Hull: Steel
Rig: Topsail schooner
Year built: 1986
Home port: Norfolk, Virginia
Flag: United States

AMERICAN ROVER

With a colorful green-and-white hull and tanbark sails, *American Rover* is easy to spot when she appears
at regattas and other events, like the Great Chesapeake Bay Schooner Race. She has an extensive day-sail
schedule out of her home port, in addition to educational field trips for students.

AMERIGO VESPUCCI

The pride of the Italian navy, *Amerigo Vespucci* conjures up memories of men-of-war from two centuries ago. Riding high in the water, with triple decks indicated by painted stripes, *Amerigo Vespucci* is a gracious twentieth-century goodwill ambassador, as well as a symbol of Italy's global maritime heritage and tradition.

Named for the great explorer and cartographer of the seventeenth century, this elegant, full-rigged ship is a grand visitor to many ceremonial parades of sail. Since her launch, *Amerigo Vespucci* has been used to train junior officers of the Italian navy.

SCANTLINGS
Length overall: 330'
Beam: 50' 9"
Draft: 23' 6"
Hull: Steel
Rig: Ship
Year Built: 1931
Home port: La Spezia, Italy
Flag: Italy

ANGELE ALINE

Built according to one of the traditional fishing vessel designs of the northern coast of France, *Angele Aline* is actually a dundée, or ketch-rigged vessel, with a retractable bowsprit that allows extra maneuverability in channels and inlets. At the turn of the century a small fleet of such dundées was based in the old fishing village of Fécamp, on the northern coast of France. *Angele Aline* was part of that fishing fleet for ten years. She fished Scottish waters for herring and, later in the season, the sea off Normandy. Eventually she was sold to a Belgian shipbuilder. During World War II she was requisitioned by the French navy as part of the evacuation of British troops at Dunkirk. *Angele Aline* now proudly displays a commemorative plaque that identifies her as part of the fleet of Dunkirk Little Ships.

In the early 1980s she was purchased by George and Muriel Thurstan, who refitted and restored her. She remains a private vessel in charter service. For the past decade she has participated in tall ship gatherings on both sides of the Atlantic.

SCANTLINGS
Length overall: 79'
Beam: 16' 5"
Draft: 9'
Hull: Wood
Rig: Ketch
Year Built: 1921
Home port: London, England
Flag: United Kingdom

SCANTLINGS
Length overall: 130'
Beam: 24'
Draft: 11'
Hull: Steel
Rig: Ketch
Year Built: 1980
Home port: Camden, Maine
Flag: United States

A N G E L I Q U E

Designed specifically to serve the tourist trade as a windjammer, *Angelique* is ketch-rigged and built to be swift, comfortable, and safe.
With her tanbark sails and a mainmast that rises 100 feet above deck, *Angelique* is a familiar sight along the "Down East" coast of
Maine. With all her sails set before the wind she recalls the nineteenth-century trawlers of the North Sea and English Channel.

A N N A   K R I S T I N A

One of the oldest vessels in the international fleet, *Anna Kristina* was built near Kristiansand, Norway, in 1889. Local pine forests were the source of some six hundred trees that provided wood for her keel and planking.

Anna Kristina is known as a *hardanger jakt,* after the fjord area in Norway where such vessels were first built. Because they were usually built and owned by farmers who had substantial supplies of timber, these vessels were solidly constructed. *Anna Kristina* has a double hull of Norwegian pine and a full frame, with timbers spaced 1 to 4 inches apart.

Hardanger jakts were rigged as sloops or ketches. *Anna Kristina* is rigged as a ketch, with her mizzenmast between the galley and the captain's cabin. She carries a square topsail. Her sails were traditionally made from cotton or flax and tanned to preserve them against the mildew and rot to which natural fibers are susceptible, hence their yellow-brown color. The twentieth century has prevailed, however, and *Anna Christiana's* sails are now made from a synthetic fiber, Duradon, which makes them lighter and more manageable than those of cotton or flax. Their traditional coloring, however, has been retained.

SCANTLINGS
Length overall: 108' 5"
Beam: 21'
Draft: 9' 6"
Hull: Wood
Rig: Ketch
Year built: 1889
Home port: Tenerife, Canary Islands
Flag: Norway

ANN CHRISTINE

A small, classic Baltic schooner, the *Ann Christine* is more than a century old. Built in 1894 by Sorenson & Sons in Ålborg, Denmark, she is currently in private service to an owner in Tunisia and operates on the North African coast of the Mediterranean. Originally christened *Ellen Margrethe* in 1894, then *Christine* in 1920, *Hansa* in 1968, and *Christine of Travemunde* in 1978, she was registered as *Ann Christine* in Panama in 1980.

A true working vessel, the *Ann Christine* has hauled cargo in traditional ways, but she has also served as a milk boat, delivering and receiving milk on the islands off the Danish coast and has also been a stone-fisher, clearing the channels and passages of the Danish islands for navigation.

Refitted seven years ago in Germany with hydraulic steering and central heating, *Ann Christine* became even more maneuverable with the addition of a bow-thruster. She received new sails at that time but maintained her fore-and-aft rigging, though she still carries one yard for a square foresail in the manner of a traditional European *galleass* rig.

SCANTLINGS
Length overall: 57' 6"
Beam: 17' 6"
Draft: 7' 9"
Hull: Wood
Rig: Schooner
Year built: 1894
Home port: Oran
Flag: Tunisia

ANTIGUA

The three-masted *Antigua* is not a new vessel. She was converted from a deepsea trawler. Acquired by the Holland's Glorie charter group of Rotterdam, the Netherlands, she underwent an extended refitting and conversion from 1993 to 1995 and emerged as a three-masted barquentine. With sixteen cabins, *Antigua* can accommodate up to thirty-two passengers for charters or sail training.

SCANTLINGS
Length overall: 158'
Beam: 24'
Draft: 11'
Hull: Steel
Rig: Barquentine
Year built: 1956
Home port: Rotterdam
Flag: The Netherlands

SCANTLINGS
Length overall: 102'
Beam: 21' 6''
Draft: 6' 6''
Hull: Steel
Rig: Brig
Year built: 1994
Homeport: Stavoren
Flag: The Netherlands

APHRODITE

Construction of this trim brig was completed in 1993. Named for the mythological goddess of beauty and love, in Greek Aphrodite means "foam-born" or sprung from the sea. Today's *Aphrodite* provides private charter service in Dutch waters.

ASGARD II

Asgard II upholds Ireland's proud and heroic maritime tradition. The original *Asgard* was owned and commanded by the Irish patriot Robert Erskine Childers (1870–1922). Childers was the author of the fabled novel, *Riddle of the Sands* (1903) and, as an accomplished sailor, was said to have smuggled guns aboard *Asgard* for the nationalist cause. Childers received the boat as a wedding present from Dr. Hamilton Osgood of Boston, Massachusetts, the father of his bride, Molly. The vessel's design was based on the work of Norwegian naval architect Colin Archer, whose ships were famous for their speed and maneuverability. The name *Asgard* comes from Norse legend and means "home of the gods," or the Elysian fields, the place of rest after death for the blessed.

The original vessel was purchased in 1964 by Coiste An Asgard, the Irish sail training organization, and preserved as an historic vessel. Found to be unseaworthy in 1974, she was transferred in 1979 to her now-permanent dryland berth, the Kilmainham Jail Historical Museum near Dublin.

Asgard II has been involved in full-time sail training since her launch in 1981. She too carries an historic Irish connection. Her figurehead is an effigy of Gráinne Mhoal, "Grace of the cropped hair," a legendary sixteenth-century Irish female sea captain and, some say, pirate. Also known as Grace O'Malley, this legendary figure purportedly found the gates of Castle Howth shut, kidnapped the heir to the castle in retaliation, and returned him only on condition that the gates never be locked at dinnertime and that a place always be laid for her at the table.

SCANTLINGS
Length overall: 104'
Beam: 21'
Draft: 9' 6"
Hull: Wood
Rig: Brigantine
Year built: 1981
Home port: Dublin
Flag: Ireland

TS ASTRID

This proud ship began as a Dutch vessel in 1918. She was acquired by Swedish owners in 1937 and renamed *Astrid*. After extensive service by various owners as a fishing vessel and then as a cargo vessel, she was acquired by the *Astrid* Trust in 1984. She then underwent five years of extensive refitting and retooling and emerged as a smart-looking brig. She now represents the southwest coast of England and in particular the city of Weymouth.

TS *Astrid* sponsors programs for youth and regularly makes appearances at major tall ship gatherings around the north Atlantic.

SCANTLINGS
Length overall: 137' 6"
Beam: 22'
Draft: 8' 3"
Hull: Iron
Rig: Brig
Year built: 1918
Home port: Weymouth, England
Flag: United Kingdom

SCANTLINGS
Length overall: 61'
Beam: 17' 6"
Draft: 9' 6"
Hull: Wood
Rig: Ketch
Year built: 1937
Home port: Öckerö
Flag: Sweden

ASTRID FINNE

Built in 1937 to join the famed fleet of the Norwegian ship rescue service, Norska Sjöröddningssällskapet, *Astrid Finne* carried sail number RS-43. She served in northern Norwegian waters until 1954, when she was acquired by the Swedish government to serve as a rescue and auxiliary service ship in the waters off Gotland.

In 1987, *Astrid Finne* was acquired by the school sailing association Mot Bättre Vetande, which means "toward better knowledge." She sails with her companion school ship, *Hawila,* providing youth fourteen to eighteen years of age a formal secondary school education together with a sail training program.

ATLANTICA

One of two ketches run by the Swedish group SKS Seglarskola, *Atlantica* was built in 1981 to be a sister ship to the agency's other vessel, *Gratitude*. She carries twenty-four youngsters on sail training cruises in the Baltic and North Seas.

SCANTLINGS
Length overall: 117'
Beam: 21' 6"
Draft: 11' 6"
Hull: Wood
Rig: Ketch
Year built: 1981
Home port: Göteborg
Flag: Sweden

ATLANTIS

SCANTLINGS

Length overall: 186'

Beam: 24' 6"

Draft: 16' 6"

Hull: Steel

Rig: Barquentine

Year built: 1905

Home port: Lübeck, Germany

Flag: Malta

Built in 1905 as the *Bürgermeister Bartels,* she ultimately served for eighty years as the *Elbe II* lightship, stationed at the mouth of the Elbe River. *Atlantis* was converted to her present rig in 1984–85. As with other lightship conversions (see also *Alexander von Humboldt* and *Europa*), beauty–and the choice of an ideal rig–was in the eye of the beholder. In this case, the beholder was Capt. Hartmuth Paschburg, who planned *Atlantis* to be a traditional barquentine. In 1986 her sail plan was reduced, and the fore-royal sail and the main gaff sail were removed; finally, the gaff-topsail and main gaff were removed leaving only her square sails and staysails.

The *Atlantis* is German-owned and usually operates as a charter vessel in the Baltic and North Seas, although she has visited warmer waters for charter work. She has accommodations for fifteen crew members and thirty-four passengers.

BALTIC BEAUTY

Built originally as a motor trawler, *Baltic Beauty* fished the Baltic Sea for more than half a century. She then caught the eye of Victor Gottlow, who acquired her in 1978. It was this new owner-captain's dream to convert his engined workhorse into an elegant two-masted schooner.
Baltic Beauty finally underwent an extensive three-year conversion that began in 1987. She emerged as a passenger-carrying sailboat, the *Dominic Fredion*. With a rough-hewn figurehead, she was renamed *Baltic Beauty* in her most recent service.

SCANTLINGS
Length overall: 131'
Beam: 16'
Draft: 9' 6"
Hull: Steel
Rig: Gaff-rigged schooner
Year built: 1926; converted, 1980
Home port: Ronneby
Flag: Sweden

BELEM

Launched in 1896 for a South American freighter service, the *Belem* carried cocoa beans from Belem, Brazil, for a Paris chocolate maker. In 1913 she was purchased by the Duke of Westminster and converted to a yacht. A decade later, she was sold to Sir A. E. Guinness, renamed *Phantom II,* and rerigged as a staysail schooner. In 1979 she was acquired by the Association for the Preservation and Protection of Old French Ships, now the Belem Foundation, and restored as a barque.

SCANTLINGS
Length overall: 167'
Beam: 29'
Draft: 12' 6"
Hull: Steel
Rig: Barque
Year built: 1896
Home port: Nantes
Flag: France

BILL OF RIGHTS

Operated by VisionQuest National Ltd. of Exton, Pennsylvania, *Bill of Rights* serves as a sailing camp for the training and education of troubled youth. Based on the "vision quest"–a challenging wilderness experience originally devised as a rite of passage to adulthood among the Plains Indians of North America, the present program combines theoretical and practical education for the students on board. The basic tenets of sail training, the development of a sense of responsibility, rigorous self-discipline, and a respect for authority are the goals of the rite of passage experienced on *Bill of Rights* today.

For the first two decades of her career, *Bill of Rights* served as a private charter yacht out of Newport, Rhode Island, and was a frequent visitor to many American ports and islands on the eastern seaboard. Built along classic schooner or clipper lines, her masts are set at a distinct rake, which establishes her aggressive but graceful profile.

SCANTLINGS
Length overall: 136'
Beam: 24'
Draft: 9' 6"
Hull: Wood
Rig: Gaff-rigged schooner
Year built: 1971
Home port: Philadelphia, Pennsylvania
Flag: United States

BLACK JACK

In 1954 Capt. Thomas G. Fuller of Ottawa purchased the steam tugboat *G. B. Patee II* from the Upper Ottawa Improvement Company. The tug, which was built in Scotland in 1904, had served for fifty years hauling logs. After an extensive refit, the vessel was transformed into a brigantine, renamed *Black Jack,* and operated as a private vessel.

In 1984, the new brigantine *Fair Jean* joined *Black Jack* to form the "fleet" of sail training vessels operated by Bytown Brigantine, Inc., of Ontario, Canada. The program offers sail training programs to youth in the Great Lakes area and the Caribbean.

SCANTLINGS
Length overall: 87'
Beam: 14'
Draft: 6'
Hull: Steel
Rig: Brigantine
Year built: 1904; converted, 1954
Home port: Ottawa, Ontario
Flag: Canada

BLACK PEARL

Completed in 1950 using surplus wood originally intended for the construction of World War II submarine chasers, *Black Pearl* crossed the picturesque entrance to Wickford Harbor on Narragansett Bay, Rhode Island, for years. Her clean, miniature lines added a new gloss to Coleridge's phrase from the *Rime of the Ancient Mariner* about a "painted ship upon a painted ocean" as she sat at anchor off Wickford.

In the late 1950s she was purchased by Barclay H. Warburton III, who sailed her to Kiel, Germany, in 1972 as the American representative to the tall ship events in Europe that summer. In 1973, Barclay founded the American Sail Training Association (ASTA), for which *Black Pearl* served as flagship.

Only 79 feet in sparred length, she is classified as an A-II vessel and is the smallest tall ship having square sails. *Black Pearl* is now operated by the Aquaculture Foundation of Bridgeport, Connecticut, as a sail training vessel.

SCANTLINGS
Length overall: 79'
Beam: 15'
Draft: 9'
Hull: Wood
Rig: Brigantine
Year built: 1951
Home port: Bridgeport, Connecticut
Flag: United States

BLUENOSE II

The original *Bluenose* was the symbol and pride of Canadian shipbuilding and sailing skill. Her image was reproduced on the country's coins and stamps, and her reputation as a sleek, fast vessel in the North Atlantic was recognized around the globe. *Bluenose II* was built in 1921. She worked and raced the waters of the northern Atlantic until 1942, when she was sold for service as a freighter in the West Indies. She foundered on a reef off the coast of Haiti in 1946.

Bluenose II is a replica of the famous schooner, built in 1963 at the same Lunenburg yard as the original *Bluenose*. Today she serves as a representative of goodwill for the province of Nova Scotia.

A survey made several years ago reported that she had serious structural problems that would force her retirement. A second survey, however, resulted in a more optimistic assessment. As a result, and with the establishment of the *Bluenose II* Preservation Trust (a registered charity that receives volunteer, government, and provincial support), an extensive and permanent plan to maintain *Bluenose II* was established.

In 1995, *Bluenose II* was fully restored by the Trust and now pursues an active sailing schedule in Nova Scotian and neighboring waters. Her home port is the Lunenburg yard where she was built.

SCANTLINGS
Length overall: 161'
Beam: 27'
Draft: 16'
Hull: Wood
Rig: Schooner
Year built: 1963
Home port: Lunenburg, Nova Scotia
Flag: Canada

BOA ESPERANZA

A replica of the fifteenth-century caravels that carried the Portuguese flag throughout the Mediterranean Sea, the south Atlantic, and the Indian Ocean, *Boa Esperanza*–"good hope"–was built and is maintained by APORVELA, the sail training association of Portugal. The most familiar caravel in the world is probably *Niña*, one of three ships that sailed in 1492 on Christopher Columbus's fateful journey of exploration. *Niña* was the smallest of the three ships and remained a *caravela latina* until square sails were added for stability on the ocean crossing and she became a *caravela rotunda.* Caravels originated in the Mediterranean and served largely as trading vessels from the fourteenth to the seventeenth centuries. Caravels have simple curved stems and plain transoms and are frequently lateen-rigged with long, tapering triangular sails. (Aficionados should note that there is not necessarily a relationship between the flush planked hulls we now refer to as *carvel*-built and the hulls of five centuries ago.) Caravels were used for the great explorations of Bartholomew Diaz in 1488 and Ferdinand Magellan's circumnavigation of 1519–22.

SCANTLINGS
Length overall: 78'
Beam: 21' 6"
Draft: 10' 6"
Hull: Wood
Rig: Lateen
Year built: 1990
Home port: Lisbon
Flag: Portugal

HMS BOUNTY

The HMS *Bounty* was built in Lunenburg, Nova Scotia, in 1960 from the same admiralty plans used for the construction of Captain Bligh's original *Bounty* of 1788. The HMS *Bounty* starred in the 1962 MGM movie *Mutiny on the Bounty,* starring Marlon Brando and Trevor Howard. After serving as an MGM exhibit in St. Petersburg, Florida, she was acquired–along with her movie rights–by Turner Broadcasting.

After an extensive search and negotiations for an appropriate recipient, the full-rigged ship was donated to the chamber of commerce of Fall River, Massachusetts, where she became part of the Maritime Heritage Park, which includes the battleship USS *Massachusetts.* Though Captain Bligh would surely recognize her, this contemporary *Bounty* boasts two Caterpillar diesels for auxiliary power and modern navigation systems, as well as safety features that meet current U.S. Coast Guard standards.

HMS *Bounty* now serves the Fall River community under the auspices of the Tall Ship *Bounty* Foundation. The *Bounty* has an integrated education program with the middle-school system of Fall River and also offers sail training.

SCANTLINGS
Length overall: 169'
Beam: 30'
Draft: 13'
Hull: Wood
Rig: Ship
Year built: 1960
Home port: Fall River,
Massachusetts
Flag: United States

BOWDOIN

A veteran of several scientific cruises into Arctic waters, this trim schooner was constructed with a specially reinforced hull to withstand the freezing grip of the icepack. After floundering between owners and restoration projects, *Bowdoin* has now found a more permanent home in Castine, Maine, with the Maine Maritime Academy. This sturdy, snub-nosed vessel serves as a classroom for high school students and educators studying marine and nautical sciences.

SCANTLINGS
Length overall: 101'
Beam: 21'
Draft: 10'
Hull: Wood
Rig: Schooner
Year built: 1921
Home port: Castine, Maine
Flag: United States

SCANTLINGS
Length overall: 145'
Beam: 24' 6"
Draft: 9' 6"
Hull: Wood
Rig: Topsail schooner
Year built: 1984
Home port: Dana Point, California
Flag: United States

CALIFORNIAN

Californian is a full-scale re-creation of the nineteenth-century Revenue Marine Service cutter *C. W. Lawrence,* which was the first cutter assigned to the California coast. *Californian* was built by the Nautical Heritage Society at Spanish Landing, San Diego. Launched in May 1984, the vessel was christened and dedicated by Gloria Deukmejian, the wife of then-governor George Deukmejian. *Californian* exemplifies the speed and elegance of the Revenue Marine Service cutters of the past and the safety and service of present-day sail training school ships.

Designated by the California legislature as the official tall ship ambassador for the state of California, this topsail schooner has been active at special events throughout the state. Starting in the spring in northern California, she generally returns to southern waters by the end of summer.

The primary purpose of *Californian* is to serve as a special sail training vessel for fourth- through eighth-grade students, senior high school students, and college and university students of the entire state. While teaching the art and skill of sailing tall ships, *Californian* also provides an environment for students to experience self-reliance and teamwork.

CAPITAN MIRANDA

When launched in 1930 in Spain, *Capitan Miranda* began her career as a cargo vessel. She then served as a hydrographic survey ship for Uruguay's navy until 1978. Since that year the vessel has undergone a major refit and rededication as a school ship. With staysail schooner rigging and a clipper bow, *Capitan Miranda* was designed for speed and looks more like a private yacht than a traditional sail training ship.

The ship is named for the renowned hydrographer and educator Capt. Francisco P. Miranda (1868–1925), who served Uruguay as an officer, cabinet official, and war and navy secretary. He finished his distinguished career as professor of marine geography at the Naval Academy of Uruguay.

SCANTLINGS
Length overall: 205'
Beam: 27'
Draft: 12'
Hull: Steel
Rig: Staysail schooner
Year built: 1930
Home port: Montevideo
Flag: Uruguay

CAROLA

Built in 1900, *Carola* is an example of the hardy wooden vessel known in northern European waters as a galleass. These gaff-rigged ketches were typical trading vessels used to transport dry cargo between ports on the Baltic Sea, hence the classification Baltic trader. *Carola*'s hull was modified to carry wet cargo in 1926; as a *well smack,* water flowed through her hull. She was restored to her original design in 1969 and is now maintained by her proud owner, Capt. Hans Edwin Reith.

Carola participates frequently in tall ship gatherings on both sides of the Atlantic.

SCANTLINGS
Length overall: 82' 2"
Beam: 16'
Draft: 6'
Hull: Wood
Rig: Gaff ketch
Year built: 1900
Home port: Travemünde
Flag: Germany

CHRISTIAN RADICH

Christian Radich was a successful businessman and shipowner of Danish descent who died childless in 1889. He stipulated in his will that 50,000 kroner should be donated for the purpose of building a sail training ship for the youth of Norway. The funds were to be released only after the death of his wife, who lived on for twenty-seven years. By that time, the initial endowment had grown to 106,000 kroner, an amount large enough to provide much of the capital of the entire building fund. When the ship was finally christened in 1937, it was appropriate that it bear the name of its prescient donor, Christian Radich.

The *Christian Radich* is owned and administered by Østlandets Skoleskib, the East Coast Training Ship, although Norway's Ministry of Education is responsible for its operating expenses. For the past decade sail training has been integrated into the official Norwegian school system. Its basic curriculum is a full ten months of education for fifty cadets ranging in ages from eighteen to twenty-four; in addition, eighteen cooks become part of the training class. Generally, the coed ratio on board is forty-six males to forty-two females.

SCANTLINGS
Length overall: 205'
Beam: 36'
Draft: 15'
Hull: Steel
Rig: Ship
Year built: 1937
Home port: Oslo
Flag: Norway

SCANTLINGS
Length overall: 76'
Beam: 11'
Draft: 11'
Hull: Steel
Rig: Staysail schooner
Year built: 1977
Home port: Hamilton
Flag: Bermuda

CHRISTIAN VENTURER

Built in 1977 as a working schooner, *Christian Venturer* originally carried a junk rig with lugsails. Converted in the 1980s to a staysail schooner, she has represented the island of Bermuda at many tall ship events. Designed and owned by William Nash and Richard Doe, *Christian Venturer* hosts a variety of sail training and educational programs. This versatile schooner also serves occasionally as a research vessel exploring the waters off the Bermuda coast and in the Gulf Stream.

CLEARWATER

This replica recalls an era when ships powered by sails provided the primary mode of transportation on the Hudson River, which joins the Atlantic Ocean at New York City. Hudson River sloops, originally based on old Dutch designs, were single-masted, shallow-draught, centerboard boats that carried passengers and cargo. Until early in the nineteenth century they carried square topsails, but ultimately triangular topsails proved more manageable. Because river sailing often requires frequent tacking or gybing, a sloop may change tacks more easily than other rigged vessels. A gybe–used when changing course while sailing before the wind–causes the boom to swing from one side of the vessel to the other. If executed carelessly a gybe can result in torn sails, damage to rigging, injury to crew, and in extreme cases a dismasting.

Clearwater is owned and operated by Hudson River Sloop *Clearwater,* Inc., a nonprofit membership dedicated to defending and restoring the Hudson River and related waterways. The organization sponsors educational programs that focus on environmental and ecological issues. *Clearwater*'s distinctive figurehead is a graceful Canada goose.

CLIPPER CITY

Clipper City is a replica of a nineteenth-century coasting schooner that carried coal and lumber between American ports on the east coast. Adapted for the twentieth century, this 158-foot topsail schooner has a steel hull instead of the wooden one of her namesake and predecessor.

With her clipper bow and square topsails, *Clipper City* recalls the famed clipper ships that made Baltimore a sailing and mercantile center of the nineteenth century, sending ships to and from the Californian gold fields and expanding trade in the West Indies and South America.

Clipper City is owned by a private chartering agency and provides daily tours of the historic harbor and upper Chesapeake Bay. She also participates in major maritime festivals along the east coast of the United States.

SCANTLINGS
Length overall: 158'
Beam: 27'
Draft: 6' 6"
Hull: Steel
Rig: Topsail schooner
Year built: 1985
Home port: Baltimore, Maryland
Flag: United States

CONCORDIA

A steel-hulled barquentine, *Concordia* was built to serve as the flagship of Canada's Class Afloat Foundation. Operating from regional headquarters on both the Atlantic and Pacific coasts, *Concordia* offers a full-time scholastic program as part of extended voyages between the North and South Pacific and the Atlantic and the Caribbean Oceans. On her maiden voyage in 1992 she participated in the Grand Columbus Regatta. After voyages to the South Pacific from her base in Vancouver, British Columbia, *Concordia* has returned to Atlantic waters and her eastern home at West Island College in Pointe Claire, Quebec.

SCANTLINGS
Length overall: 185'
Beam: 30'
Draft: 13' 2"
Hull: Steel
Rig: Barquentine
Year built: 1992
Home port: Quebec
Flag: Canada

SCANTLINGS
Length overall: 204'
Beam: 43' 6"
Draft: 22' 5"
Hull: Wood
Rig: Ship
Year built: 1797
Home port:
Boston, Massachusetts
Flag: United States

USS CONSTITUTION

The most famous and most enduring tall ship in America, the USS *Constitution* was one of six warships commissioned by President George Washington to protect the young nation's maritime interests and shores. Authorized by Congress in 1794, she was built at Edmund Hartt's shipyard near Boston's Old North Church. The copper for many of her fittings came from a mill operated by patriot Paul Revere.

The ship was so large that some sailors doubted she would be of practical value, but she proved herself both strong and fast (with a top speed of 13.5 knots). Her original specifications put her at 204 feet long overall (175 feet on the waterline) and gave her thirty-six sails with an area of 42,270 square feet, forty-four guns (although she often carried fifty) with a range of 1,200 yards, and a crew of 450. She was completed in 1797 at a cost–including her figurehead, which represents Hercules with a raised club–of $320,718.84.

Thwarting Barbary pirates in the Mediterranean and repelling French privateers in the Caribbean, *Constitution* proved to be an eminently serviceable vessel. She earned her legendary nickname, Old Ironsides, in the War of 1812 when British frigates were frustrated to see their cannonballs bounce off her 21-inch oak-planked hull.

After serving as the flagship of the American fleet in the Mediterranean, *Constitution* was removed from active service in 1828. Two years later, the U.S. Navy judged her unseaworthy. She was saved only by congressional intervention after an outcry of public support, spurred by publication of the poem "Old Ironsides," by Oliver Wendell Holmes. She was rebuilt in 1855, restored in 1871, and served as a Navy training ship for several years before her active career came to an end. Largely forgotten, she sat decomposing at a pier in the Portsmouth, New Hampshire, Naval Shipyard. There was a proposal to tow her to sea as a target for gunnery practice. After appropriating limited money for repairs in 1906, Congress finally agreed to supplement the money raised by school children from around the United States to pay for a complete rebuilding of *Constitution* between 1927 and 1930. Then, on 2 July 1931, towed by a mine sweeper, *Constitution* began a national tour that took her from Maine to Washington through the Panama Canal. She called on ninety ports and received some 4.5 million visitors. Three years later, she took up a permanent station at the now-retired Boston Naval Shipyard in Charlestown, Massachusetts, where she remains the nation's oldest ship in active commission and a national historic landmark.

Old Ironsides "sails" Boston harbor annually for her maintenance turnaround; she is turned so that her port and starboard sides weather evenly at dockside. During the past decade this event has been scheduled to coincide with gatherings of the international tall ship fleet in Boston Harbor. *Constitution* underwent her most recent major refitting and restoration in preparation for marking the celebration of her bicentennial year in 1997.

CORONET

One of the great private yachts of the gilded age of the turn of the century, *Coronet* circumnavigated the globe twice, raced for international cups, and served as a missionary vessel for a Christian fellowship.

Built to rigorous standards in 1885, *Coronet*'s design called for a "plumb stem," structural strength, and speed. Keel, keelson, frames, and planks were all of white oak from Maine. In addition to the pine of her cabin ceilings, the finest teak was used for her stanchions, and mahogany of exceptional density and grain from Honduras was fashioned for the brightwork of her rails and deckhouses. At the height of her sailing career in the 1890s she was owned by Newport philanthropist Arthur Curtis James and went on to serve as flagship for the New York Yacht Club.

After a hundred years of sailing she was recently acquired by the International Yacht Restoration School, which was founded by Elizabeth Meyers. Returned to Newport, Rhode Island, an extensive restoration program has begun to return *Coronet* to her former glory.

SCANTLINGS
Length overall: 133'
Beam: 27'
Draft: 12' 6"
Hull: Wood
Rig: Schooner
Year built: 1885
Home port:
Newport, Rhode Island
Flag: United States

CORWITH CRAMER

Corwith Cramer is a 134-foot steel-hulled brigantine designed specifically to meet the requirements of accredited programs for high school and college-level students run by the Sea Education Association in Woods Hole, Massachusetts. *Corwith Cramer* is one of two vessels that fulfills the at-sea portion of SEA's programs in oceanography and marine science.

The other vessel, *Westward,* was built as a private yacht. Her design and sheer were incorporated into the more functional design of *Corwith Cramer,* which was built in 1987 in Bilbao, Spain, to the design specifications of Woodin & Marean of Wiscosset, Maine.

SCANTLINGS
Length overall: 134'
Beam: 26'
Draft: 13'
Hull: Steel
Rig: Brigantine
Year built: 1987
Home port: Woods Hole,
Massachusetts
Flag: United States

CREOLE

One of the most beautiful and biggest private yachts ever made, *Creole* has had a varied career that has seen her ownership shift between some of the wealthiest sailing families in the world and fledgling educational programs for disadvantaged youth. From the Greek shipping magnate Stavros Niarchos, her fortunes brought her to the Nyborg Sail Training School in Denmark. In the past decade millions of dollars have been spent to refurbish her to her former elegance by the Gucci family of Italy, but her present situation remains uncertain.

SCANTLINGS
Length overall: 215'
Beam: 31'
Draft: 19'
Hull: Steel
Rig: Staysail schooner
Year built: 1927
Home port: Uncertain
Flag: Italy

SCANTLINGS
Length overall: 221'
Beam: 32' 6"
Draft: 15' 6"
Hull: Steel
Rig: Schooner
Year built: 1937
Home port: Lisbon
Flag: Portugal

CREOULA

Creoula is a four-masted, steel-hulled schooner built in 1937 in a record sixty-two workdays. She was constructed for a Portuguese fishing company, Parceria Geral de Pescarias, and until her last trip in 1973, *Creoula* had wooden topmasts, booms, and gaffs. The standing rigging has always been steel, and the running rigging was originally made from sisal rope.

Until 1973, this four-masted schooner spent thirty-seven consecutive years working the cold waters off Grand Banks, Newfoundland. The ship typically set sail from Lisbon in April for Nova Scotia, where she remained until the end of May. After renewing supplies in Sidney, Nova Scotia, or St. John's, Newfoundland, *Creoula* would sail to Greenland, where she fished until mid-September, often reaching a latitude of 48° off the western coast of Greenland. If her holds were not full, she fished again off Newfoundland until mid-October and then returned to Portugal with 800 tons of salted fish and 60 tons of cod-liver oil. At the fishing grounds she launched one-person dories. Often the fishers took dogs with them; their barking helped *Creoula* to find them in the fog.

In 1979 she was purchased from the Portuguese Department of Fisheries with the intention of converting her to a museum of fishery. A survey showed her hull to be in impeccable condition, however, and a decision was made to restore her as a sail training vessel. She is now owned by the Portuguese navy but carries only civilian cadets and trainees.

In 1992, *Creoula* was modified slightly, and a portion of the original crew's quarters amidship was converted to a classroom and library.

CUAUHTEMOC

Named for the last of the Aztec emperors, this new barque represents the Mexican navy. *Cuauhtemoc* is one of four barques built for Latin American nations to serve as goodwill ambassadors and training schools for their respective navies. The other members of the quartet are *Gloria* of Columbia (1968), *Guayas* of Ecuador (1977), and *Simon Bolivar* of Venezuela (1980). Last of the four, built in 1982, *Cuauhtemoc* was constructed in the famed shipyard Astilleros y Talleres Celaya, S.A., Bilbao, Spain.

SCANTLINGS
Length overall: 270'
Draft: 17' 1"
Beam: 39' 4"
Rig: Barque
Hull: Steel
Home port: Acapulco
Flag: Mexico

DANMARK

Danmark is a familiar visitor to the United States. This 249-foot ship serves the Danish Marine Authority from her home port in Copenhagen.

On a visit to New York in 1939, *Danmark*'s captain, Knud Hansen, offered the services of the ship to the United States. Hansen wanted to avoid surrendering her to Axis powers and to ensure her safety during the war years. During World War II, *Danmark* served as a school ship at the U.S. Coast Guard Academy in New London, Connecticut, training future Coast Guard and Navy officers. After the war, she was sailed back to Denmark, but a few Danes returned to the United States and made their homes in the New London area. Several of them assisted the Coast Guard in sailing a similar vessel, a barque, USCGC *Eagle*, formerly *Horstwessel*, from Bremerhaven, Germany, to the United States.

A model of the *Danmark*, symbolizing her service to the United States, graced the Oval Office during the presidency of John F. Kennedy.

SCANTLINGS
Length overall: 253'
Beam: 33'
Draft: 15'
Hull: Steel
Rig: Ship
Year built: 1933
Home port: Copenhagen
Flag: Denmark

DAR MLODZIEZY

SCANTLINGS
Length overall: 360'
Beam: 45' 9"
Draft: 20' 7"
Hull: Steel
Rig: Ship
Year built: 1982
Home port: Gdynia
Flag: Poland

Dar Mlodziezy ("gift of the children") is a full-rigged, 360-foot ship designed by the distinguished Polish naval architect Zygmunt Choren and is the flagship of the Merchant Marine Academy (Wyzsza Szkola Morska) in Gdynia, Poland. *Dar Mlodziezy* was funded in part by the contributions of elementary school children during the 1960s and 1970s. Commissioned in 1982, she replaced the venerable *Dar Pomorza* ("gift of Pomorze," a reference to the coastal region of Poland), which served Poland for more than six decades before her retirement. *Dar Pomorza* participated in Operation Sail in 1976.

Dar Mlodziezy's distinctive design served as the prototype for a class of vessels (five in all) built in Gdansk for the Russian confederation of the 1980s. Four of the five vessels–*Mir, Druzhba, Pallada,* and *Nasheba*–now fly the Russian flag, while *Khersones* flies the flag of Ukraine. These are true sister ships and vary only slightly in dimensions and configuration.

SCANTLINGS
Length overall: 148'
Beam: 21' 4"
Draft: 11' 6"
Hull: Wood
Rig: Schooner
Year built: 1902
Home port: Vamdrup
Flag: Denmark

DEN STORE BJORN

Den Store Bjorn takes her name from the great bear constellation. Originally built as a lightship in 1902, *Den Store Bjorn* was towed to a fixed position and therefore did not have an engine, although she was refitted with one in 1959. Finally taken out of navigational service, she was bought in 1980 by the Danish Schooner Cooperative. She is now operated by Smaskolen Fremtidens Danmark/Sofolkene (Small School for Future Danish Seafolk), and she carries five permanent officers and crew members, three teachers, and twelve trainees, ranging in ages from sixteen to twenty.

In addition to practical courses in seamanship and the marine sciences, students receive instruction in the compulsory curriculum of the Danish elementary school system.

DEWARUCI

Originally ordered from a German yard in 1932, *Dewaruci's* construction was delayed by the advent of World War II until the yard itself, heavily damaged, could be repaired. Finally completed two decades later, *Dewaruci* is a barquentine and functions as a sail training vessel for the Indonesian navy. Her figurehead and name represent the mythological Indonesian god of courage and sincerity. Sailing from her home port in the Indian Ocean, *Dewaruci* makes the longest journeys of any vessel to participate in the American and European tall ship events.

SCANTLINGS
Length overall: 191'
Beam: 31'
Draft: 13'
Hull: Steel
Rig: Barquentine
Year built: 1952
Home port: Jakarta
Flag: Indonesia

SCANTLINGS
Length overall: 295'
Beam: 39'
Draft: 17'
Hull: Steel
Rig: Barque
Year built: 1936
Home port: New London,
Connecticut
Flag: United States

EAGLE

Flagship of the U.S. Coast Guard Academy, *Eagle* also serves as an international goodwill ambassador for the United States. *Eagle's* primary mission is training U.S. Coast Guard cadets in the fundamental disciplines of seamanship. Through practical application, cadets learn navigation, engineering, and ship maneuvering. In addition, they set some 20,000 square feet of sail and control more than 20 miles of rigging lines while under way.

The *Eagle* was originally named *Horst Wessel* and was one of four German sister training ships built in the famous Blohm & Voss shipyard in Hamburg during the 1930s. She came under the U.S. flag at the conclusion of World War II. Her sister ships, still part of the international fleet, are *Sagres II* (Portugal), *Mircea* (Romania), *Tovarishch* (Ukraine), and *Gorch Fock II* (Germany), built in 1958 from the same plans and design as the *Eagle.*

Today, *Eagle's* home port is New London, Connecticut, but she is just as likely to be seen in ports and harbors around the world representing the United States at tall ship gatherings and other international events.

SCANTLINGS
Length overall: 181'
Beam: 40' 6"
Draft: 16' 6"
Hull: Steel
Rig: Schooner
Year built: 1989
Home port: Scheveningen
Flag: The Netherlands

EENDRACHT II

Eendracht II, which means "unity" in Dutch, combines state-of-the-art yacht racing technology, such as self-furling sails, and an emphasis on traditional teamwork and discipline for her cadets. A fast, modern replacement for the older sail training vessel of the same name, *Eendracht II* includes state-of-the-art comforts like air conditioning and deep-freeze food lockers for future Dutch naval officers in training.

E L E N A – M A R I A – B A R B A R A

A replica of the nineteenth-century schooners that sailed the waters of the eastern Baltic Sea, *Elena–Maria–Barbara* is a tall ship with a Russian perspective. Considerably smaller than the barques and fully rigged ships in the Russian fleet, *Elena–Maria–Barbara* appears almost tiny by comparison, but she represents a hardy class of sailing vessel that operated out of St. Petersburg a century ago. Note her exaggerated jibboom, which extends more than 30 feet from her bow. This vessel was built and is supported by an avid sailing club in St. Petersburg.

SCANTLINGS
Length overall: 97'
Beam: 16'
Draft: 8'
Hull: Wood
Rig: Schooner
Year built: 1992
Home port: St. Petersburg
Flag: Russia

ELINOR

Built in 1906 at Stubbekøbing, Denmark, *Elinor* carries and sets some specialized sails. Although technically a schooner, she crosses one yard for her square foresail and often sets two raffe sails (a raffe is a triangular, square-rigged topsail) from the topmast to the yard. In addition, she often changes her hull color to match her charter assignments: a traditional black hull for the Baltic and northern waters and a white hull for her time in the Caribbean.

SCANTLINGS
Length overall: 118'
Beam: 19' 6"
Draft: 7'
Hull: Wood
Rig: Schooner
Year built: 1906
Home port: Copenhagen
Flag: Denmark

SCANTLINGS
Length overall: 202'
Beam: 28'
Draft: 16'
Hull: Iomore iron and welded steel
Rig: Barque
Year built: 1877
Home port: Galveston, Texas
Flag: United States

ELISSA

The pride of the Galveston Historical Foundation, *Elissa* is one of the few remaining iron-hulled vessels still sailing. She enjoyed a long career as a cargo vessel, which saw her registered under six different flags, beginning in Scotland in 1877 and ending as a demasted motor vessel in the Greek Islands. Her hull was found in the Mediterranean awaiting a scrapper's acetylene torch by the late archaeologist Peter Throckmorton, through whose efforts and advocacy she was purchased by the foundation in 1975. *Elissa* was brought to Texas in 1979 and now makes Galveston–a port she had visited under other flags more than a century ago–her home port.

ERNESTINA

Originally named *Effie M. Morrissey, Ernestina* began as a Grand Banks, Newfoundland, fishing schooner. After twenty-five years of service, she was acquired by Capt. Robert Bartlett, who used her for Arctic exploration in 1925. Over the next twenty years she served in northern waters and even held a commission in the United States Navy during World War II.

After the war, under the helm of Capt. Henrique Mendes, she made more than twelve passages from the Cape Verde Islands to the United States carrying cargo and immigrants. A sturdy wooden-hulled schooner, *Ernestina* sailed through many storms, but none compared with the treacherous difficulties she experienced in recent years trying to survive and sustain herself. At one point, precarious finances prompted a crew to abandon the vessel at dockside in Miami, Florida.

In 1982 she was donated by the Republic of Cape Verde to the people of the United States, her title to be held by the Commonwealth of Massachusetts. In recognition of her distinguished history and service, *Ernestina* is now an historic landmark. Berthed at New Bedford, Massachusetts, she is used to present historical, educational, and maritime programs.

SCANTLINGS
Length overall: 156'
Beam: 25'
Draft: 13'
Hull: Wood
Rig: Schooner
Year built: 1894
Home port: New Bedford, Massachusetts
Flag: United States

ESMERALDA

The pride of the Chilean navy, *Esmeralda* was built in Cadiz, Spain, from plans used to build Spain's *Juan Sebastian de Elcano*. Both vessels were constructed from a Camper & Nicholson design at the same yard, though some twenty-seven years apart–Echevarrieta y Larriñaga in Cadiz. The only differences between these two elegant four-masters are the additional fore-and-aft sail on the *Sebastian's* foremast, designating her as a topsail schooner, and the slightly flatter angle of *Esmeralda's* bowsprit.

Esmeralda was completed in 1954. Her distinctive figurehead represents a giant Andes condor, the national bird of Chile.

SCANTLINGS
Length overall: 371'
Beam: 42' 8"
Draft: 19' 8"
Hull: Steel
Rig: Four-masted barquentine
Year built: 1952-54
Home port: Valparaiso
Flag: Chile

ETOILE MOLENE

Appearing to be a gaff ketch, this 115-foot wooden vessel is proudly called a Dundée thonier by her captain, Robert Escoffier, of St. Mâlo. She is distinguished from other European ketches by her retractable bowsprit. Built in 1954, she wears the traditional yellow sails of the Brest region of France. Her name means "star of Molene" and refers to a snug harbor near Brest, France.

SCANTLINGS
Length overall: 115'
Beam: 21' 4"
Draft: 12' 6"
Hull: Wood
Rig: Dundée thonier
Year built: 1954
Home port: St. Mâlo
Flag: France

EUROPA

This charming barque exudes Old World warmth and ambiance and is another of the many conversions to sail made in recent decades. Originally a lightship in the North Sea, *Europa* is now a commercial charter vessel sailing from Rotterdam. She is named for the Greek mythological figure Europa, who infatuated the god Jupiter with her beauty. He appeared to her as a lovable bull and carried her off to Crete. After bearing him two children, Jupiter named the continent of Europe in her honor. *Europa's* figurehead depicts the legendary beauty whose name she carries.

Built in 1911 in Hamburg, Germany, *Europa* was acquired in 1987 and rebuilt for her recent service as a private charter vessel. Operating out of the Netherlands, *Europa* makes worldwide sailing passages with fifty passengers.

SCANTLINGS
Length overall: 180'
Beam: 24' 6"
Draft: 12' 6"
Hull: Steel
Rig: Barque
Year built: 1911
Home port: Rotterdam
Flag: Holland

EXCELSIOR

The Lowestoft "smack," or "dandy," is a sailing trawler with noteworthy characteristics. Its heavy construction and long, straight keel permit long stays at sea in all weather. Being deep-drafted and having a moderate ratio of beam to length make the design both "sea-kindly" and fast.

The ketch rig is unusual on smacks in that both masts are raked forward, allowing great versatility in the setting of sails. The sail plan can be varied to suit conditions, and the disposition of the sails balances the helm.

In 1971 *Excelsior* (LT 472) was serving as a motor coaster, carrying cargo around Norway. She was acquired by the *Excelsior* Trust with the intention of making her an active, seagoing sailing vessel. With the aid of many local firms and the sponsorship by the Manpower Services Commission in Lowestoft, a thorough renovation of her hull and upper works (including rigging) was completed in 1988.

Excelsior is tiller-steered on an open deck, though she now has bulwarks to provide safety and security at sea. Despite appearances, the traditional tan sails and running rigging are made from synthetic fibers, which are naturally colored. These lines last longer and are safer because they resist the dangers of rot and mildew associated with hemp and flax.

SCANTLINGS
Length overall: 108' 6"
Beam: 19' 3"
Draft: 8' 6"
Hull: Wood
Rig: Ketch
Year built: 1921
Home port: Lowestoft
Flag: United Kingdom

EYE OF THE WIND

This square-rigged, iron-hulled vessel was originally a topsail schooner, built for the South American hide trade in 1911. In 1923 she was sold to Swedish owners and for the next fifty years served as a Baltic trader in the Baltic and North Seas.

In 1973, *Eye of the Wind* was purchased by a private, five-member syndicate that restored and furnished her to serve as the flagship of Operation Drake in the South Pacific. Along with an appearance in the First Fleet Reenactment to celebrate Australia's centenary, this brigantine again rounded Cape Horn in December 1991 to take part in the Grand Columbus Regatta of 1992.

With her tanbark sails and colorful pennants flying from her mainmast, *Eye of the Wind* is an active and attractive addition to the international fleet of tall ships. Her figurehead is a "wind cherub," designed and carved by one of her original partners, Rodney Clarke, of Redfern, Australia. Along with the spirit of adventure of the crew, the cherub is a welcome addition to this striking brigantine-brig. She is often square-rigged on one or both of her masts. *Eye of the Wind* starred in the recent movie *White Squall*.

SCANTLINGS
Length overall: 132'
Beam: 23'
Draft: 9'
Hull: Iron
Rig: Brigantine
Year built: 1911
Home port: Faversham, Kent
Flag: United Kingdom

FAIR JEANNE

A new brigantine designed by the late Capt. Thomas G. Fuller, this 110-foot brigantine is the most recent addition to the sail training fleet of Bytown Brigantine, Inc., of Ontario, Canada. She serves as a sail training vessel for young adults and provides a floating classroom for secondary school classes. Since her launch in 1982 *Fair Jeanne* has participated in many of the major tall ship regattas in North America. She is named for the wife of Captain Fuller, Jeanne Fuller.

SCANTLINGS
Length overall: 110'
Beam: 24' 6"
Draft: 6' or 13'
Hull: Steel and fiberglass
Rig: Brigantine
Year built: 1982
Home port: Kingston, Ontario
Flag: Canada

SCANTLINGS
Length overall: 46'
Beam: 10' 6"
Draft: 4' 6"
Hull: Ferro-cement
Rig: Junk schooner
Year built: 1978
Home port: Solomon's Island, Maryland
Flag: United States

FOON YIN

This singular junk-rigged schooner is made from ferro-cement. Her name means "welcome" in Chinese.
Combining unique materials with a unique rig, *Foon Yin* is an example of the infinite variations seen in both old
and new sailing vessels. Her Chinese red lugsails are a colorful addition to many seascapes.

FRYDERYK CHOPIN

This elegant brig is named for the nineteenthcentury Polish composer and pianist. Designed by the naval architect Zygmunt Choren to the specifications of Capt. Krysztof Baranowski, *Fryderyk Chopin* combines maximum sail area and speed with stability and safety for educational programs. Measuring 182 feet long overall, with masts soaring 125 feet above her deck, *Fryderyk Chopin* is rigged to carry six jib sails along with its high skysails.

The filigree of her standing rigging and the number of sails she carries make *Fryderyk Chopin* ideal for sail training and require concentrated effort from her disciplined crews. On her maiden voyage and first Atlantic crossing in 1992, she participated in Operation Sail in New York and also visited Boston, Massachusetts, and Newport, Rhode Island.

SCANTLINGS
Length overall: 182'
Beam: 28'
Draft: 12' 6"
Hull: Steel
Rig: Brig
Year built: 1992
Home port: Szczecin
Flag: Poland

GALAXY

Built in 1960 at a yard in Portugal by owner Brian Street, this trim brigantine sails from a home port on the Red Sea. Initially a charter boat in the Mediterranean, *Galaxy* has operated from several Israeli ports. Under the helm of Brian Street she has served as the flagship for the state of Israel at the past two Operation Sail events in the United States. Asked about his reasons for building a brigantine, Street quoted an old Hebrew saying, "Fools never die, they just change places" and added that he has long been a fool over square-riggers.

SCANTLINGS
Length overall: 125'
Beam: 23'
Draft: 13'
Hull: Wood
Rig: Brigantine
Year built: 1960
Home port: Eilat, Israel
Flag: Israel

GAZELA PHILADELPHIA

Built in Portugal in 1883 as the *Gazela Primerio,* this 178-foot barquentine worked the Grand Banks fishing grounds off Newfoundland for nearly a century before her acquisition and restoration by the Ship Preservation Guild of Philadelphia. She is the oldest wooden square-rigger still in active service.

During her fishing career she carried a crew of forty men to the Grand Banks, where thirty-five one-person dories rowed out to net cod. Each day the fish caught were cleaned, salted, and stored until the ship's 350-ton capacity was reached and the six-month voyage completed.

The ship was originally constructed of two types of pine, "stone" pine and "marine" pine, which were cultivated for their qualities of close-grain and hardness in special forests planted by order of Prince Henry the Navigator in the fourteenth century.

In Philadelphia she hosts programs on ship preservation, sail training, and marine science for youngsters and volunteers. *Gazela Philadelphia* is the city's maritime ambassador to national and international events, and she also serves as a museum of sailing ship technology.

SCANTLINGS
Length overall: 178'
Beam: 27'
Draft: 17'
Hull: Wood
Rig: Barquentine
Year built: 1883
Home port: Philadelphia, Pennsylvania
Flag: United States

GEORG STAGE

Two small fully rigged ships have carried the name *Georg Stage*. The first was built in 1882 and is now moored at Mystic Seaport in Connecticut. She was renamed the *Joseph Conrad* by the famed Australian sea captain Alan Villiers. The present *Georg Stage* is a fully rigged ship built between 1934 and 1935 at the Fredrikshavn shipyard in northern Denmark. Both ships were named in honor of Georg Stage, who died at the age of twenty-two. He was the son of Danish boat builder Frederik Stage. The original ship's figurehead, which portrays the young Georg Stage, was transferred to the ship, which now carries his name.

Georg Stage is primarily engaged in training young men and women for careers in maritime service. Under the administrative office of the Georg Stage Memorial Foundation, the ship provides an environment where "young people can acquire practical maritime skills at sea in situations where teamwork and mutual respect are essential; after which they can decide if life at sea will suit them."

Measuring a trim 178 feet from bowsprit to stern, she is the smallest fully rigged ship in the world.

SCANTLINGS
Length overall: 178'
Beam: 27' 6"
Draft: 13'
Hull: Iron plates
Rig: Ship
Year built: 1935
Home port: Copenhagen
Flag: Denmark

GLADAN AND FALKEN

These twin schooners were built in the same yard and according to the same plans in 1947.
Differentiated only by their sail numbers, S01 for *Gladan* and S02 for *Falken,* these two vessels
train future officers of the Swedish royal navy as they have since their commissioning.

SCANTLINGS
Length overall: 129'
Beam: 23'
Draft: 13' 9"
Hull: Steel
Rig: Schooner
Year built: 1947
Home port: Karlskrona
Flag: Sweden

SCANTLINGS
Length overall: 76'
Beam: 17'
Draft: 4' 6"
Hull: Wood
Rig: Schooner
Year built: 1989
Home port: Biloxi, Mississippi
Flag: United States

GLEN L. SWETMAN

Glen L. Swetman is a replica oyster schooner–one of two–built by the Biloxi Schooner Project for the Maritime and Seafood Industry Museum. She was launched in 1989. Her sister ship, *Mike Sekul,* was completed in 1994.

Biloxi schooners are specific to the fertile but shallow estuarine waters of the Mississippi Sound. The shallow draft, broad beam, and great sail area of the Biloxi schooner allowed it to dredge oysters in less than 6 feet of water and then virtually fly back to Biloxi at 12–14 knots with its heavy load under a cloud of sail. During the off season, these schooners raced one another competitively, a tradition that has been renewed at the annual Race of the White Wings, which is sponsored by the Maritime and Seafood Industry Museum.

G L O R I A

Built to train future officers of the Colombian navy, *Gloria* recalls the great sail training barque of the 1930s, though she was one of four barques built during the 1960s and 1970s at the famous Astilleros y Talleres Celaya shipyard in Bilbao, Spain.

The concept of a training ship was promoted by three influential Colombian leaders: naval commander Admiral Orlando Lemaitre Torres; defense minister General Gabriel Rebeiz Pizarro; and project director Commander Benjamin Alzate Reyes. After her keel was laid in 1967, *Gloria* was completed in 1968. General Rebeiz died before the ship was christened, and as a gracious tribute to his efforts, to ensure that this important project reached completion, the vessel was named Gloria, for his wife, Gloria Zawadsky de Rebeiz.

Gloria carries a crew of ten officers, a professional crew of fifty, and sixty to seventy-five cadets on her extensive training cruises in the north and south Atlantic.

SCANTLINGS
Length overall: 249'
Beam: 34' 8"
Draft: 16' 4"
Hull: Steel
Rig: Barque
Year built: 1968
Home port: Cartegna
Flag: Colombia

SCANTLINGS
Length overall: 293'
Beam: 39'
Draft: 15' 6"
Hull: Steel
Rig: Barque
Year built: 1958
Home port: Kiel
Flag: Germany

GORCH FOCK II

Built from the same plans and in the same shipyard (Blohm & Voss in Hamburg, Germany) as the original, *Gorch Fock II* boasts contemporary safety features and the latest navigational equipment. She is an eminent replacement for her namesake (now the training vessel *Tovarishch* from Ukraine). Since her launch in 1958, *Gorch Fock II* has logged thousands of nautical miles in her twice-yearly voyages and has hosted more than ten thousand cadets for training cruises.

The barque is named for a popular German writer of sea stories, Hans Kinau (1880–1916), who used the pseudonym Gorch Fock (fock means "foresail" in German). Kinau became part of the romantic mythology of the sea when he perished aboard the cruiser *Weisbaden,* which was sunk during the Battle of Jutland on 31 May 1916.

Gorch Fock II is a proud symbol of Germany's distinguished sailing and shipbuilding traditions.

LA GRANVILLAISE

A traditional bisquine, *La Granvillaise* is rigged with lugsails often used in the province of Brittany. With her foremast in "the eyes," a retractable bowsprit and the quadrilateral shapes of her sails (heads narrower than feet and luffs shorter than leeches), *La Granvillaise* presents a distinctive profile.

For centuries the towns of Granville and Cancale competed commercially on the waters of Mont St. Michel bay in Normandy. In the nineteenth-century a fierce but friendly rivalry began between the fishing fleets of the two harbors, which added to the anecdotal folklore. To restore this heritage and to preserve the tradition of the local bisquines, the town of Cancale built *Cancalais* in 1987; the town of Granville followed with *La Granvillaise* in 1990. Today, these fishing vessels add an aesthetic and historic dimension to the bay they share.

SCANTLINGS
Length overall: 40'
Beam: 11'
Draft: 8'
Hull: Wood
Rig: Bisquine
Year built: 1990
Home port: Granville
Flag: France

SCANTLINGS
Length overall 257'
Beam: 33'
Draft: 14' 6"
Hull: Steel
Rig: Barque
Year built: 1977
Home port: Guayaquil
Flag: Ecuador

GUAYAS

The figurehead of a giant Condor distinguishes *Guayas* of Ecuador from her sister ship, *Gloria* of Columbia. Built in Spain in 1977, *Guayas* was commissioned for the training of cadets and junior officers of the Ecuadorian Naval Superior School at Guayaquil. The school, which was founded by Simón Bolívar in 1822, is located on the River Guayas, from which the ship takes her name.

Guayas is home to the 63 trainees on each of her cruises, with an additional complement of 110 crew and officers. The Ecuadorian navy still considers sail training essential to developing a spirit of teamwork in the country's young sailors.

HARVEY GAMAGE

A typical coastal schooner, *Harvey Gamage* is a virtual sister vessel of *Bill of Rights*. Both are identified by their large mainsails as they visit the waters of the northeast Atlantic. *Harvey Gamage* is named for the distinguished master shipwright from Maine, Harvey Gamage. She is a beautiful tribute to the shipbuilder's art and an example of the coastal vessels that plied the waters of the east coast a century ago carrying commercial cargo.

For the twenty-first century her purpose has been redefined. Under the auspices of a new nonprofit foundation, the Schooner *Harvey Gamage* Foundation of Francestown, New Hampshire, the schooner provides educational programs which use the power of the sea and the challenge of the sailing ship to lead students of all ages to intellectual and personal growth. The *Harvey Gamage* Sea Education programs are structured adventure expeditions integrated with academic studies in marine science, literature, arts and humanities, math and history. During the fall and spring semesters, *Harvey Gamage* serves as a sailing classroom for the Ocean Classroom program run in conjunction with Proctor Academy. Open adult programs are available during the summer in New England waters and during mid-winter in Caribbean waters.

Harvey Gamage sails with a permanent crew of seven to ten members, along with twenty-five students.

SCANTLINGS
Length overall: 131'
Beam: 23' 6"
Draft: 10'
Hull: Wood
Rig: Schooner
Year built: 1973
Home port: Bath, Maine
Flag: United States

HAWAIIAN CHIEFTAIN

With a design that recalls the traditional ketches of northern European coastal traders, *Hawaiian Chieftain* makes her home in Sausalito, California, and in the northern waters of California. Built at Lahina, Maui, in 1988 as a charter vessel, this topsail ketch has relocated to San Francisco Bay to offer a full program of sail training, vessel handling, and environmental studies as well as corporate charters and day sails.

The steel hull is 65 feet long, and *Hawaiian Chieftain* is sparred to a length of 103 feet from the tip of her bowsprit to the end of her mizzenboom. She carries eleven sails, totaling 4,200 square feet of canvas and uses more than ninety lines to set her sails.

Hawaiian Chieftain is a splendid blend of the old and the new. She sails at a very low angle of heel, and with a draft of 5 feet she is able to navigate in shallow coastal waters.

In addition to serious educational programs, this ketch carries "water balloon" cannons, which provide her students an opportunity for gunnery practice when encroaching vessels come into range.

SCANTLINGS
Length overall: 103'
Beam: 22'
Draft: 5' 6"
Hull: Steel
Rig: Topsail ketch
Year built: 1988
Home port: Sausalito, California
Flag: United States

HAWILA

A 121-foot traditional Baltic ketch, *Hawila* sails frequently to tall ship events in the Baltic and North Seas. She is typical of the many black-hulled Baltic traders that have been converted to serve in sail training programs for youngsters. Asked about the meaning of her name, one crew member claimed that *Hawila* was named for an accurate Swiss watch, though he admitted in passing that her name also had a biblical allusion. In the story of Genesis, the river that watered the garden of Eden branched into four streams afterward. The first branch encircled all the land of "Havilah . . . where the gold is." The gold of Havilah was frankincense.

Hawila's wooden hull was completed in 1935. She was purchased by her present owner, the sailing association Mot Bättre Vetande, in 1978 and was rebuilt into a school sailing ship by young people who volunteered their time. She finally began her career as a school sailing ship in 1984. Her season generally runs from 1 May until the end of October. About four hundred trainees, ages fourteen to eighteen, sail aboard *Hawila* each year.

SCANTLINGS:
Length overall: 121'
Beam: 21' 6"
Draft: 10'
Hull: Wood
Rig: Ketch
Year built: 1935
Home port: Öckerö
Flag: Sweden

HENRYK RUTKOWSKI

Discovered as an abandoned hull along the Polish coast at the end of World War II, the *Henryk Rutkowski* had served as a German coastal cutter, or *kriegsfishkutter,* before the war. She was rebuilt in 1951 as a gaff ketch and served as a school ship for young fishers. In 1986 she underwent a second major refitting and rerigging and emerged as a brigantine serving the fishery shipyard Szkuner. She now represents the Polish Yachting Association and serves as a sail trainer for handicapped and troubled youth. With her characteristic maroon sails, *Henryk Rutkowski* is a distinctive 94-foot ship with a professional crew of four and a crew of twenty-one student cadets.

SCANTLINGS
Length overall: 94'
Beam: 21'
Draft: 10' 6"
Hull: Wood and steel
Rig: Brigantine
Year built: 1944;
refitted, 1951 and 1986
Home port: Gdansk
Flag: Poland

HOSHI

With elegant sheer lines and rigging more typical of a private yacht, *Hoshi* displays her lineage as a Camper & Nicholson design. After a number of private owners, she became the flagship of the Island Cruising Club (ICC) of Devon in 1958. For close to sixty years ICC has provided sail training and adventure cruises in and around England and neighboring waters with *Hoshi* and other vessels.

Hoshi, Japanese for "shooting star," has accommodations for twelve, including the skipper, mates, and cook.

SCANTLINGS
Length overall: 86'
Beam: 14' 2''
Draft: 8' 6''
Hull: Wood
Rig: Schooner
Year built: 1909
Home port: Salcombe, England
Flag: United Kingdom

INLAND SEAS

Inland Seas is a floating classroom outfitted with scientific equipment that enables students to study the Great Lakes ecosystem. The schooner is equipped with state-of-the-art navigational instruments and is a U.S. Coast Guard-certified passenger vessel. *Inland Seas* is staffed by a professional crew of mariners and educators.

SCANTLINGS
Length overall: 80'
Beam: 17'
Draft: 7'
Hull: Steel
Rig: Schooner
Year built: 1994
Home port: Suttons Bay, Michigan
Flag: United States

ISKRA

Ikra, which in Polish means "spark" (as in "to spark a flame"), is named for an historically important Polish schooner of the early twentieth century. The first *Iskra* was a wooden, three-masted schooner that trained more than four thousand officers for the Polish navy in her fifty years of service, from 1927–77. The new *Iskra* carries the name ORP *Iskra* (Officers Reserve of Poland) in honor of the Westerplattes Heroes Naval Academy of Gdynia which she represents.

Another of the many vessels designed by Zygmunt Choren, *Iskra* proudly flies the navy ensign and represents the Republic of Poland on official visits.

SCANTLINGS
Length overall: 161'
Beam: 26'
Draft: 11' 6"
Hull: Steel
Rig: Barquentine
Year built: 1982
Home port: Gdynia
Flag: Poland

SCANTLINGS·
Length overall: 106'
Beam: 21'
Draft: 10' 6"
Hull: Wood
Rig: Brigantine
Year built: 1957
Home port: Leith, Scotland
Flag: United Kingdom

JEAN DE LA LUNE

Built as a motor trawler in 1957, *Jean de la Lune* served as part of the tuna fleet out of the Azores for a number of years. In the mid-1970s she was bought and refurbished in Colchester, England. She emerged as a staysail schooner and served briefly in the charter trade.

In 1988 she was acquired by her present owner, John Reid, who envisioned her as a square-rigger. Working with a team of volunteers, Reid spent six years completing the arduous conversion of *Jean de la Lune* to a brigantine.

In 1995 she was the host vessel for the tall ship regatta in Edinburgh, or, more precisely, Leith, Scotland.

JENS KROGH

Built in 1899 at Frederikshaven near the northern tip of Denmark, *Jens Krogh* now calls Ålborg, Denmark, her home port. Converted from a fishing vessel, *Jens Krogh* trains young Danish boys and girls in the art of sailing and in the marine sciences.

Called *Ulla Vita* before she was acquired in 1973 by the FDF Skøreds (the Danish sea scouts), the group restored and then renamed her *Jens Krogh*.

SCANTLINGS
Length overall: 80'
Beam: 16' 6"
Draft: 6' 10"
Hull: Wood
Rig: Ketch
Year built: 1899
Home port: Ålborg
Flag: Denmark

SCANTLINGS
Length overall: 370'
Beam: 43'
Draft: 22' 6"
Hull: Steel
Rig: Topsail schooner
Year built: 1927
Home port: Cadiz
Flag: Spain

JUAN SEBASTIAN DE ELCANO

This graceful four-masted topsail schooner is one of the longest tall ships in the world and measures 370 feet long overall. *Juan Sebastian de Elcano* is officially the training ship for the midshipmen and ensigns of the Spanish navy.

The schooner is named in honor of Juan Sebastian de Elcano, captain of Ferdinand Magellan's last exploratory fleet. The captain returned to Seville, Spain, on 6 September 1522. The ship also carries the de Elcano coat of arms–a terraqueous globe and the motto "Primus Circumdedisti Me" (first to circumnavigate me)–which Emperor Charles I conferred on de Elcano after he returned to Spain having completed Magellan's global expedition.

Built in Cadiz, Spain, in 1927, the ship's hull was designed by the Echevarrieta y Larriñaga shipyard of Cadiz. Her rigging and sails were planned by the English sailmaker Nicholson. Both designs were used twenty-five years later to build the Chilean sail training vessel *Esmeralda* in 1952–54.

Juan Sebastian de Elcano also honors four previous sail training vessels–*Bianca, Almansa, Asturias,* and *Nautilus*–by designating her masts with their names.

KAISEI

Kaisei, which means "ocean planet," is the flagship of the Sail Training Association of Japan. She is a two-masted brigantine that will serve as Japan's first civilian sail training vessel. Her maiden voyage in 1992 extended from Gdansk, Poland, to Misaki, Japan, with a circumnavigation of Great Britain as a symbolic salute to one island nation from another and in anticipation of the ocean crossings to follow.

SCANTLINGS
Length overall: 151'
Beam: 25'
Draft: 11' 2"
Hull: Steel
Rig: Brigantine
Year built: 1991
Home port: Tokyo
Flag: Japan

KAIWO MARU II
AND NIPPON MARU II

These twin barques were built in 1984 and 1989, respectively, by the Institute of Sea Training in Japan. They replaced the venerable twins *Kaiwo Maru I* and *Nippon Maru I,* which were built in the 1930s, served as sail training vessels, and then, ignominiously, as demasted barges during World War II. The original vessels were 318 feet long. Their more modern sisters, the *Kaiwo Maru II* and the *Nippon Maru II,* are improved versions and reach 361 feet overall. They incorporate the experience of the earlier sail trainers with the demands and technological needs of the twenty-first century.

Built by Sumitomo Heavy Industries at the Uraga dockyards, the new barques are exemplary models of shipbuilding and Japanese scientific analysis. The *Kaiwo Maru II* and *Nippon Maru II* have become emissaries of culture and goodwill around the world for the Japanese people.

Both ships carry a complement of 197 officers and permanent crew and a cadet contingent of 120. Both have the same inventory of sails (thirty-six), and when before the wind the sails have an area of close to 30,000 square feet.

One innovation for these second-generation sail training vessels is the addition of graceful figureheads to their bowsprits. Ranjō is personified with her hands clasped in prayer on *Nippon Maru,* while on *Kaiwo Maru* the figure of Konjō, her younger sister, is depicted preparing to play a flute. These are demure representations of idealized Japanese womanhood whose names both mean "deep blue sea."

SCANTLINGS
(Identical for both)
Length overall: 361'
Beam: 46'
Draft: 22'
Hull: Steel
Rig: Four-masted barque
Year built: 1984/1989
Home port: Tokyo
Flag: Japan

KALIAKRA

Completed in 1984, *Kaliakra* trains future officers for the Bulgarian navy and is a sister ship to *Iskra*. Her home port is Varna on the Black Sea, although she has been a frequent participant in European and American tall ship gatherings. As initially rigged, only four yardarms crossed her foremast because of variations in deck thickness that affected the height of the foremast. Since her refitting in 1992, however, she carries five yardarms in her barquentine configuration. Her figurehead is a stylized version of a Bulgarian mythological figure.

SCANTLINGS
Length overall: 159'
Beam: 27'
Draft: 11'
Hull: Steel
Rig: Barquentine
Year built: 1984
Home port: Varna
Flag: Bulgaria

K A S K E L O T

Built in the J. Ring-Andersen yard of Svenborg, Denmark, *Kaskelot* underwent a major refit and rerigging in 1956 and emerged as the barque she is today. Built to serve the Greenland colonies as a supply ship, *Kaskelot* has been modified a number of times for her appearance in films. She has enjoyed starring roles as Capt. Michael Scott's *Terra Nova,* as Fried Nansen's *Fram,* and as *Hispaniola* in Robert Louis Stevenson's *Treasure Island.*

SCANTLINGS
Length overall: 153'
Beam: 25'
Draft: 12'
Hull: Wood
Rig: Barque
Year built: 1948
Home port: Jersey Island
Flag: United Kingdom

KHERSONES

Khersones is the fifth in a group of six full-rigged ships that were built in Gdansk, Poland, during the 1980s. The other class A vessels are *Dar Mlodziezy* (1982), *Druzhba* (1986), *Mir* (1987), *Pallada* (1989), and *Nadeshda* (1992). *Khersones* is named for the ancient port of Khersone on the Black Sea and is now operated by the Khersone Maritime Academy. She plans to make a circumnavigation that will retrace the expeditionary routes of Sir Francis Drake in the Pacific Ocean.

SCANTLINGS
Length overall: 356'
Beam: 45' 9"
Draft: 21' 7"
Hull: Steel
Rig: Ship
Year built: 1987
Home port: Khersone
Flag: Ukraine

SCANTLINGS
Length overall: 376'
Beam: 46' 1"
Draft: 23' 5"
Hull: Steel
Rig: Four-masted barque
Year built: 1926
Home port: St. Petersburg
Flag: Russia

KRUZENSHTERN

This majestic, four-masted barque is the second-largest tall ship still sailing, surpassed in length only by the other Russian four-masted barque, *Sedov*. (*Kruzenshtern* is 376 feet in overall length, to *Sedov's* overall length of 386 feet.) Both vessels are frequent visitors to the many festivals and regattas held in Europe and America.

Kruzenshtern has had a remarkable career on the seas and links present-day school ships to the magnificent cargo sailing vessels of the nineteenth and early twentieth centuries. Originally named *Padua, Kruzenshtern* was built for a famed shipbuilder and owner from Hamburg, Germany, F. Laeisz.

She made her final voyage for the famed Flying P cargo line in 1938–39, leaving Bremen, Germany, to sail to Chile for nitrates and then to Australia for wheat. The other steel-hulled vessels and four-masted barques of the famed Flying P's were: *Pommern, Pamir, Parma, Passat,* and *Peking.* Three of these Flying P's survive as museum ships around the world–*Pommern* in Marienhamn, Finland; *Passat* in Travemunde, Germany; and *Peking* at the South Street Seaport Museum in New York City, making *Kruzenshtern's* continued voyages all the more remarkable.

During World War II her hull was ignominiously used as a barge. At the end of hostilities, she was transferred to the Soviet fleet and assigned to the Soviet Ministry of Fisheries as a training vessel. At that time she was renamed *Kruzenshtern* to honor the late eighteenth- and nineteenth-century sailor, circumnavigator, and oceanographer Adam Johann Ritter von Kruzenshtern (1770–1846). During the period 1959–61 she received a major refit and twin diesel engines.

She flies the Russian flag, with a registry in St. Petersburg, once von Kruzenshtern's home. Owing to her particular history and construction, she has received grants from the German Republic to underwrite her maintenance and recent major refits. Before the wind, her four masts carry foresails measuring more than 36,584 square feet, which make an awesome display of sail power.

LADY MARYLAND

"Pungy" schooners were an indigenous and plentiful craft on the waters of and around the Chesapeake Bay. Throughout the nineteenth century these colorful ships served to dredge oysters and to transport commercial goods between many small ports along the bay. To commemorate these vessels, the Living Classroom Foundation of Baltimore has constructed a full-sized, authentic representation of these turn-of-the-century tall ships and created the two-masted, gaff-rigged pungy schooner *Lady Maryland*. Her green and pink colors are traditional.

Along the eastern seaboard of the United States from Maryland to Maine, this floating classroom has engaged students and youth in the study of marine science, ecology, and sailing. Beyond sail training, participants aboard *Lady Maryland* can learn everything from vocational skills, such as woodworking and marine mechanics, to such traditional classroom subjects as math and science. In addition, curricula have been developed for the study of the Chesapeake Watershed, the marine life in surrounding estuaries, and the natural resources of the area.

Lady Maryland also participates in programs with the Living Classroom's Maritime Institute, which is working toward the restoration of Maryland's historic skipjack fleet. Her educational programs are supported by private corporations, the city of Baltimore, and the state of Maryland.

SCANTLINGS
Length overall: 104'
Beam: 22'
Draft: 7'
Hull: Wood
Rig: Schooner
Year built: 1986
Home port: Baltimore, Maryland
Flag: United States

SCANTLINGS
Length overall: 112'
Beam: 22'
Draft: 11'
Hull: Wood
Rig: Brig
Year built: 1989
Home port: Aberdeen, Washington
Flag: United States

LADY WASHINGTON

In 1787 Capt. Robert Gray sailed the ranging tender *Lady Washington*, together with *Columbia Rediviva*, from Boston, Massachusetts, on the first exploration of the uncharted waters of America's Pacific Northwest. The voyage led to the "discovery" and naming of Oregon's Columbia River and Gray's Harbor in Washington. On a later voyage, *Lady Washington* was the first ship to fly the American flag in Japan.

The current *Lady Washington* is a full-scale reproduction that duplicates the original to the extent that historical records and U.S. Coast Guard regulations permit. She is the largest square-rigged sailing vessel on the Pacific coast and among other statistics boasts more than three miles of traditional rope rigging.

Built primarily from old-growth Douglas fir, *Lady Washington* was launched in 1989. She is a frequent visitor to harbors and maritime festivals up and down the Pacific Northwest and sails from Seattle during the summer months. She serves as the flagship of Gray's Harbor Historical Seaport in Aberdeen, Washington.

STS LEEUWIN II

STS *Leeuwin II* is named for the Dutch vessel that charted the southwestern corner of continental Australia in the seventeenth century. The Dutch word *leeuwin* means lioness. The effort to construct a sail training vessel for western Australia was aided by the enthusiasm and attention drawn to the region by Alan Bond's capture of the America's Cup in 1983. Completed in 1986, *Leeuwin II* participated in the defense of the America's Cup off Fremantle in 1987 as well as in Australia's bicentennial celebration in 1988.

Through most of the sailing season, STS *Leeuwin II* schedules ten-day sail training cruises for groups of young people. She is maintained and operated by the Leeuwin Ocean Adventure Foundation Ltd. of Fremantle.

SCANTLINGS
Length overall: 180'
Beam: 30'
Draft: 11'
Hull: Steel
Rig: Barquentine
Year built: 1986
Home port: Fremantle
Flag: Australia

LENE MARIE

A classic Baltic trader, *Lene Marie* is rigged as a ketch, popular in Danish waters and the Baltic Sea. She carries two cutter-raked masts (stepped at an angle, rather than standing perpendicular), with a mizzenmast shorter than the main. Baltic traders are handsomely designed with heart-shaped sterns and beautiful profiled and scrolled name boards. Her unusual plum-colored hull is an innovative derivation from her original fire-engine red hull under the Danish flag. While undergoing a haul for regular bottom mainte-nance there was a shortage of red paint to coat her hull, so black enamel was added, and the mixture resulted in her distinctive plum-purple finish. As proof of her heartiness, this wooden vessel completed a world circumnavigation between 1980 and 1988. *Lene Marie* is privately owned.

SCANTLINGS
Length overall: 105'
Beam: 20'
Draft: 8'
Hull: Wood
Rig: Ketch
Year built: 1810
Home port: Newport, Rhode Island
Flag: United States

SCANTLINGS
Length overall: 75'
Beam: 15' 2"
Draft: 4' and 8' 6"
Hull: Wood and epoxy
Rig: Schooner
Year built: 1993/94
Home port: Key West, Florida
Flag: United States

LEOPARD

Distinctive in plan and rigging, *Leopard* is the "dream schooner" of her designer and owner, Reuel Parker. She is built on the lines of the pilot schooner known as No. 17, which was cataloged by the French naval "constructor" and historian Jean Baptiste Marestier in 1821. The original design is similar to a Baltimore clipper, with a hull deeper aft than forward, sharply raked masts, and substantial sail area for extra speed. Parker combined the swift and seaworthy lines with a centerboard to create a vessel that is both stable in deepwater and can navigate in waters as shallow as 4 feet. *Leopard* is rigged with an overlapping lug-foresail and masts raked aft 10° from vertical.

Pilot schooners reflect an indigenous American design that evolved from the early schooners of the American Revolution to the Baltimore Clippers of the mid-nineteenth century. These vessels served as blockade runners, privateers, revenue cutters, slavers, men-of-war, and pilot schooners. Their designs promoted speed and weatherliness. Pilot schooners employed a simple rigging that permitted easy, single-handed sailing from the offshore Atlantic in all types of weather after discharging pilots to harbor-bound ships. The *Leopard* demonstrates these sailing characteristics, and her name, taken from the novel *The Snow Leopard,* by Peter Matthiessen, furthers her association with speed and agility.

LETTIE G. HOWARD

The keel of this hardy, wooden fishing schooner was laid down in the Essex, Massachusetts, shipyard of A. D. Story in 1893. Built for a local angler, Capt. Fred Howard, the schooner was named for his daughter, Lettie G. Howard, who had celebrated her twenty-second birthday that year. The design of this vessel echoes the classic "Fredonia" design of Edward Burgess. His *Fredonia,* of 1889, was the prototype for schooners of the late nineteenth century. With their graceful clipper bows these vessels were attractive but also fast and seaworthy under way.

The *Lettie G. Howard* was acquired by the South Street Seaport Museum in New York in 1968. Extensive restoration and rebuilding were completed on the "Lettie's" centenary in 1993, and in celebration she sailed to ports along the east coast.

SCANTLINGS

Length overall: 125'
Beam: 8' 4"
Draft: 10' 6"
Hull: Wood
Rig: Schooner
Year built: 1893; restored, 1993
Home port: New York, New York
Flag: United States

LIBERTAD

This full-rigged ship represents the Argentine navy. At 356 feet in overall length, *Libertad* is one of the longest sailing ships in the world. A popular visitor to American and European ports and maritime festivals, *Libertad* participated in Operation Sails in 1964, 1976, 1986, and 1992. On one of her transatlantic crossings in 1966 she used all 28,500 square feet of her sails to set a new record–eight days and twelve hours–crossing the North Atlantic between Cape Race, Canada, and the English Channel, a record that still stands. Her figurehead is a sculpture that depicts Liberty, for which the ship is named.

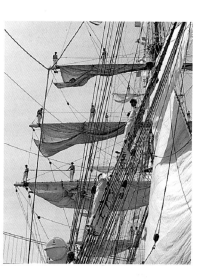

SCANTLINGS

Length overall: 356'
Beam: 45' 3"
Draft: 21' 9"
Hull: Steel
Rig: Full-rigged ship
Year built: 1960
Home port: Buenos Aires
Flag: Argentina

LIBERTY CLIPPER

Purchased and relocated to Maine in 1995, *Liberty Clipper* is designed along the lines of nineteenth-century Baltimore clippers and recalls those popular vessels of the Chesapeake Bay. Originally, *Liberty Clipper* was a day charter vessel and operated for many years from Mystic, Connecticut. Then named *Mystic Clipper,* she was a familiar site on Long Island and Block Island Sounds.

In 1995 she was acquired by Sail, Inc., of Bath, Maine, and is one of two vessels offering programs collectively called Ocean Classroom.

SCANTLINGS
Length overall: 125'
Beam: 26'
Draft: 7' 6"
Hull: Steel
Rig: Schooner
Year built: 1983
Home port: Boston,
Massachusetts
Flag: United States

LINDEN

Linden was built in Åland, Finland, in 1992. Based on the lines and fame of the original schooner named *Linden*, built in 1920, the new three-masted schooner recalls another century, although her safety features, including steel bulkheads, prepare her for the twenty-first century. The contemporary *Linden* was built by a group of sailing enthusiasts and artisans who sought to maintain the ship building tradition of the Åland Islands.

Linden is close to nature and her past. She is constructed of pine with Swedish tar between her planks. Her masts and bowsprit are of larch from the legendary forests of Kitee and Punkaharju in Finland. These "mast forests" were planted by Czar Alexander II in 1880 for future shipbuilding. Masts fashioned from these trees display characteristics common to the living trees: enduring strength.

SCANTLINGS
Length overall: 157' 6"
Beam: 28'
Draft: 9'
Hull: Wood
Rig: Schooner
Year built: 1992
Home port: Mariehamn
Flag: Finland

LORD NELSON

In 1978 the Jubilee Sailing Trust of Great Britain commissioned Colin Mudie to create a sail training vessel with specific characteristics and design features. The vessel was intended to provide a traditional sailing experience for able-bodied sailors while enabling physically challenged people to experience the wonder and awe of the sea. The special features of *Lord Nelson* include a design to maximize sailing stiffness and reduce heel in order to minimize roll; a flat deck and elevators between decks to allow the unobstructed passage of wheelchairs and other necessary equipment; a widened platform bowsprit that allows wheelchair access to set the jibs; and elimination of unnecessary clutter on deck to permit free movement.

Lord Nelson embodies the courage and fortitude she is intended to bring to her crews. She is named after Horatio Nelson, 1758–1805, the legendary admiral of the British fleet who was mortally wounded aboard his flagship, HMS *Victory,* at the Battle of Trafalgar. Nelson's smaller fleet defeated the Napoleonic fleet of French and Spanish warships that had threatened to invade England. *Lord Nelson* was christened on 4 July 1986 and has met the needs of a special population of sailors. The ship has been so successful that the Jubilee Sailing Trust has commissioned another vessel of similar design to be built, this time reviving traditional methods to construct a sail training vessel of wood.

SCANTLINGS
Length overall: 169' 6"
Beam: 28'
Draft: 13' 6"
Hull: Steel
Rig: Barque
Year built: 1986
Home port: Southampton
Flag: United Kingdom

MALABAR

Formerly, *Rachel and Ebenezer* of the Atlantic coast, *Malabar* has found a new home in the northern Great Lakes of the American Midwest. Built in 1975 with a hull of ferro-cement, this gaff-rigged schooner now operates as one of two vessels of the Traverse Tall Ship Company of Traverse City, Michigan. Along with the schooner Manitou, *Malabar* is a familiar sight in the northern waters of Lakes Michigan, Huron, Erie, Ontario, and Superior, where she offers educational and sail training cruises as well as private charters.

SCANTLINGS
Length overall: 105'
Beam: 21'
Draft: 8' 5"
Hull: Ferro-cement
Rig: Schooner
Year built: 1975
Home port: Traverse City, Michigan
Flag: United States

MALCOLM MILLER

With the growing interest and support for the first Sail Training Association schooner, *Sir Winston Churchill,* and the need for more berths, *Malcolm Miller* was built in 1967 and launched in 1968 at the John Lewis yard in Aberdeen, Scotland. She is named for the young son of Sir James Miller, who died in a car accident when he was in his twenties. Sir James, the former lord mayor of London and provost of Edinburgh, created a living memorial to his son by providing a large portion of the building costs for the second vessel. The figurehead of *Malcolm Miller* carries the coat of arms of the Miller family. Designed and built specifically for Sail Training Association programs, in alternate years she carries all-female crews on her cruises.

SCANTLINGS
Length overall: 150'
Beam: 26' 8"
Draft: 15'
Hull: Steel
Rig: Topsail schooner
Year built: 1968
Home port: Aberdeen, Scotland
Flag: United Kingdom

MARITÉ

Abandoned on the Faeroe Islands of Denmark, *Marité*'s hull was discovered by a group of Swedish ship enthusiasts in 1977. Her hull design, a "cod's head and mackerel tail," is typical of traditional fishing vessels, and from aloft she presents a wide bow and narrower stern. The original group of five entrepreneurs rescued the hulk and over the course of several years restored her. She emerged as an attractive, three-masted topsail schooner belying the neglect and redefinition she had endured over five decades.

Built as fishing schooner in the old fishing village of Fécamp on the northern coast of France, *Marité* is now a corporate charter conference vessel out of Stockholm.

SCANTLINGS
Length overall: 154'
Beam: 26' 4"
Draft: 13' 5"
Hull: Wood
Rig: Topsail schooner
Year built: 1923
Home port: Stockholm
Flag: Sweden

MERCATOR

Mercator is a barkentine representing Belgium. She was built in 1932 at the Ramage & Ferguson yard in Leith, Scotland. As a sail training and cargo vessel on South American runs, she became the best known vessel under the Belgian flag. In 1956 she was one of the few vessels to participate in the first tall ship gathering sponsored by England's Sail Training Association.

Decommissioned in 1960, she served as a museum ship and attracted more than 3 million visitors. The year 1986 marked the beginnings of a long-term restoration and refitting, which has included renewing her wooden decks and overhauling her rigging. This enabled her to represent Belgium as the host flagship for the 1993 gathering of tall ships in Antwerp. Flying only a partial suite of sails, she led the parade of ships proudly before returning to Ostend, Belgium. There, ongoing restoration is returning her to full sail and service as a sail training vessel for the Belgian navy.

SCANTLINGS
Length overall: 257' 6"
Beam: 35'
Draft: 15' 6"
Hull: Steel
Rig: Barkentine
Year built: 1932
Home port: Ostend
Flag: Belgium

SCANTLINGS
Length overall: 358'
Beam: 45' 9"
Draft: 21' 7"
Hull: Steel
Rig: Ship
Year built: 1987
Home port: St. Petersburg
Flag: Russia

MIR

Mir, which is Russian for "peace," is one of four vessels completed in the Gdansk, Poland, shipyard for the former Soviet Union. She is a sister ship to the prototype vessel *Dar Mlodziezy* (1982) as well as *Druzhba* (1987), *Khersones* (1988), *Pallada* (1989), and *Nasheba* (1992). At 360 feet, *Mir* operates from the Marine Engineering College of St. Petersburg and offers courses in marine science and oceanography in addition to sail training.

SCANTLINGS
Length overall: 269'
Beam: 39'
Draft: 17'
Hull: Steel
Rig: Bark
Year built: 1938
Home port: Constanza
Flag: Romania

MIRCEA

The last of the quartet of sail school ships built in the Hamburg, Germany, yard of Blohm & Voss in the 1930s,
Mircea is the flagship and training vessel of the Romanian navy. *Mircea* and her sister ships became the models for
sailing vessels that incorporate a school for the training of naval and merchant marine officers. The concept was
replicated in the school ships of Latin American countries and the *Dar Mlodziezy*–class vessels built in Gdansk in
the past decade. *Mircea* is named for a fourteenth-century Romanian hero, Prince Mircea, who liberated the Black
Sea coastline from the Turks and, in doing so, established Romania's maritime heritage.

MÖWE

The uncommon Germanic design of *Möwe* is called a ewer. These vessels are flat-bottomed with a shallow draft and no keel. Though rare and almost extinct today, vessels like *Möwe* fulfilled many tasks along the northern coast of Germany and Denmark in the late nineteenth century, particularly in the shallow waters of marshlands and inlets. *Möwe* is preserved by a volunteer group affiliated with the Maritime Museum in Hamburg.

SCANTLINGS
Length overall: 50'
Beam: 13'
Draft: 4'
Hull: Wood
Rig: Ewer
Year built: 1922
Home port: Hamburg
Flag: Germany

MYSTIC WHALER

Based on the design of traditional New England trading schooners, *Mystic Whaler* visits ports along the Atlantic coast on day sails and overnight cruises during the summer season. She makes lighthouse cruises that emphasize the picturesque guardians of the New England coast, and explores the islands of Long Island and Rhode Island Sounds. *Mystic Whaler* sails with a crew of five and accommodates thirty-eight guests.

SCANTLINGS
Length overall: 110'
Beam: 25'
Draft: 7' 6"
Hull: Steel
Rig: Schooner
Year built: 1967
Home port: Mystic, Connecticut
Flag: United States

NEW WAY

Another schooner that serves as a sailing "camp" for VisionQuest National Ltd. of Exton, Pennsylvania, this vessel enjoyed a distinguished career as the vessel *Western Union*. Built in 1939, she was used to lay and maintain underwater cable for the Western Union Company. In her present assignment she is dedicated to the education and "passage" of troubled youth.

SCANTLINGS
Length overall: 132'
Beam: 23' 6"
Draft: 8'
Hull: Wood
Rig: Schooner
Year built: 1930
Home port: Exton, Pennsylvania
Flag: United States

SCANTLINGS
Length overall: 198'
Beam: 32' 6"
Draft 11'
Hull: Wood
Rig: Brig
Year built: 1988
Home port: Erie, Pennsylvania
Flag: United States

NIAGARA

The U.S. brig *Niagara* is a reconstruction of the relief flagship of Commodore Oliver Hazard Perry. On 10 September 1813, Perry led nine small ships, including *Niagara*, against a British squadron of six vessels in the Battle of Lake Erie at Put-in-Bay, Ohio. It proved to be a pivotal battle of the War of 1812 and secured the Northwest Territory, opened supply lines, and boosted the nation's morale. During the battle, Perry engaged the British ships *Detroit* and *Queen Charlotte*. After his flagship, *Lawrence*, was disabled, Perry transferred his command to the undamaged *Niagara* and hoisted his battle flag, which was inscribed with the motto, "Don't Give up the Ship."

Owned by the Pennsylvania Historical and Museum Commission, *Niagara* is a working vessel dedicated to presenting living history. Built in 1988 of wood, *Niagara* educates the public about the ships and sailors of the War of 1812. In addition, she is the official flagship of the Commonwealth of Pennsylvania and makes several goodwill appearances annually with a crew of forty, half of whom are volunteers.

NORFOLK

The skipjack *Norfolk* was built at Deal Island, Maryland, in 1900. Originally christened *George W. Collier,* she dredged oysters for many years, working under a still-applicable Maryland law that mandates that Chesapeake Bay oysters be harvested only by vessels under sail. Skipjacks were introduced in the bay in the mid-nineteenth century. They are distinguished by hulls with hard chines, large centerboards, sloop rigs, and foresails set on a bowsprit. They were a vital part of the bay's development and worked from Norfolk, Virginia, to Baltimore, Maryland. One of only a few surviving examples of skipjacks from the turn of the century, the *Norfolk* represents a significant part of the Chesapeake Bay's commercial fishing industry.

At the end of her working career, she was donated to the city of Norfolk and rechristened *Norfolk.* In 1990, she was rebuilt and refitted under the auspices of a grant to the city from the Dalis Foundation. She is now operated by the Norfolk Parks and Recreation Department in cooperation with qualified volunteers, Sea Scouts, and Nautical Adventures, Inc.

SCANTLINGS
Length overall: 71'
Beam: 15' 6"
Draft: 7' with centerboard
Hull: Wood
Rig: Skipjack
Year built: 1900
Home port: Norfolk, Virginia
Flag: United States

ÖSTERSCHELDE

A fine example of Dutch boat construction at the turn of the century, *Österschelde* has been rebuilt from her hull through her rigging. She now sails as a private charter vessel in waters worldwide. Though she began her career as a sailing vessel, she was motorized and demasted in the 1930s. Transformed from her past service as a motor coaster, *Österschelde* is the last representative of the large fleet of three-masted topsail schooners that sailed under the Dutch flag at the turn of the century. Her restoration was carried out with the cooperation of three maritime museums. On 21 August 1992 *Österschelde* was officially relaunched by Princess Margriet in Rotterdam.

SCANTLINGS
Length overall: 167'
Beam: 25'
Draft: 10'
Hull: Steel
Rig: Topsail schooner
Year built: 1918
Home port: Rotterdam
Flag: The Netherlands

PACIFIC SWIFT

Built during Expo '86 in Vancouver, British Columbia, *Pacific Swift* is the flagship of the Sail and Life Training Society (SALTS) of Victoria, British Columbia. Along with another school vessel, *Robertson II, Pacific Swift* embarks on six-month educational journeys throughout the South Pacific.

Crafted from local timbers, Alaskan cedar, and Douglas fir, *Pacific Swift* was modeled after the eighteenth-century brig *Swift*. The original *Swift* was probably built in the Canadian Maritimes, suggested by the French fleur-de-lis which decorate her transom. She was captured by the British navy and hauled out in London in 1783 for a survey. She was described as a clipper packet brig. The "clipper" designation referred to her shape; it suggests that she was designed for speed. "Packet" referred to the merchant or commercial service in which she was engaged; and "brig" described her rigging, which allowed for downwind sailing, with her two masts of square sails and a fore-and-aft sail on the mainmast to allow for more maneuverability and speed when sailing into the wind. *Pacific Swift* has added a few more fore-and-aft sails to her rig as a topsail schooner to allow for more maneuverability.

SCANTLINGS
Length overall: 111'
Beam: 20' 6"
Draft: 10'
Hull: Wood
Rig: Topsail schooner
Year built: 1986
Home port: Victoria, British Columbia
Flag: Canada

PATRICIA DIVINE

Designed by Merritt Walter and built in 1987, *Patricia Divine* is named for her owner's daughter. Though constructed using modern materials, the schooner's lines are based on the plan for a nineteenth-century British Revenue cutter.

Operating from the Chesapeake Bay, *Patricia Divine* passed her sea trials with a cruise from her home port to Bermuda and back again. She is the only vessel to have sailed in all nine of the Great Chesapeake Bay Schooner Races, which are held annually in October.

Patricia Divine combines traditional lines with elegant interior detailing to ensure that her charter and sail training voyages are as comfortable as they are instructive. Built for the luxury charter trade, she is certified to carry twenty-five day passengers and six overnight guests.

SCANTLINGS
Length overall: 69' 6"
Beam: 14' 8"
Draft: 6' 6"
Hull: Steel
Rig: Topsail schooner
Year built: 1987
Home port: Annapolis, Maryland
Flag: United States

PIONEER

A workhorse of a vessel, *Pioneer* was originally an iron-clad sloop, designated to carry raw materials on the coastal waters of New Jersey, New York, and Pennsylvania. She worked first for the Pioneer Iron Company, transporting sand to its main foundry in Chester, Pennsylvania. After being refitted with a more traditional schooner rig in 1895, *Pioneer* continued to transport coal, lumber, bricks, and eventually oil as a tanker until 1956.

In 1955, at the end of a working career of seven decades, she was sold to Russell Grinell of Gloucester, Massachusetts, who began an arduous reconstruction of her hull using steel plating and restored *Pioneer* to a traditional sailing rig. Upon his death in 1970 she was donated to New York's South Street Seaport, where *Pioneer* has continued to exemplify the nineteenth-century sailing traditions of the mid-Atlantic seaboard.

SCANTLINGS
Length overall: 102'
Beam: 21' 6"
Draft: 4' 8"
Hull: Iron and steel
Rig: Schooner
Year built: 1885
Home port: New York, New York
Flag: United States

P O G O R I A

Pogoria holds the distinction of being the first completed design for a square-rigger by Polish naval architect Zygmunt Choren. Built for the Steel Workers Union in 1980, *Pogoria* has served as the background for a movie and as a floating classroom for West Island College of Quebec, Canada. She is now the flagship of the Polish Sail Training Association in Gdansk.

Pogoria's hull design served as the model for three other vessels: *Iskra* for the Polish navy, *Kaliakra* for the Bulgarian navy, and *Oceania,* a specially rigged oceanographic research vessel from Gdynia, Poland.

SCANTLINGS
Length overall: 154'
Beam: 26'
Draft: 11' 6"
Hull: Steel
Rig: Barkentine
Year built: 1980
Home port: Gdynia
Flag: Poland

PRIDE OF BALTIMORE II

Pride of Baltimore II is a topsail schooner built to the lines of a nineteenth-century Baltimore clipper. With her clipper bow, exaggerated bowsprit, and the distinct rake to her masts, *Pride of Baltimore II* is a living part of a past era. Her mission now, however, is to carry knowledge and teach discipline to the crews of youthful students who crowd her deck. She is owned by the state of Maryland and is operated by *Pride of Baltimore*, Inc.

Pride of Baltimore II sails as a goodwill ambassador for the state of Maryland and for the city and port of Baltimore. She has successfully completed voyages to the West Coast (including Alaska and Hawaii), South America, and to European waters. She sails with two rotating captains and a crew of eleven.

SCANTLINGS
Length overall: 170'
Beam: 26'
Draft: 12' 4"
Hull: Wood
Rig: Topsail schooner
Year built: 1988
Home port: Baltimore, Maryland
Flag: United States

PROVIDENCE

Providence is a replica of one of America's most historic vessels, the sloop *Katy*. She was the first vessel selected for the Continental navy and the first command of John Paul Jones, father of the America's navy. As a Revolutionary War vessel, she carried twelve cannons and is credited with having captured or sunk more than forty foreign fighting vessels. She was the first vessel to land amphibious troops, the American marines, on foreign soil.

Providence is maintained and operated by a nonprofit foundation, Seaport '76. She was built in time for the bicentennial celebrations of 1976 and since then has logged thousands of miles representing the nation, the state of Rhode Island, and the city of Newport at domestic and international maritime celebrations.

SCANTLINGS
Length overall: 110'
Beam: 20'
Draft: 10'
Hull: Fiberglass and wood
Rig: Square-sail sloop
Year built: 1976
Home port: Newport, Rhode Island
Flag: United States

SCANTLINGS
Length overall: 91'
Beam: 20'
Draft: 4' 6"
Hull: Wood
Rig: Gaff schooner
Year built: 1984
Home port: New Haven,
Connecticut
Flag: United States

QUINNIPIACK

A two-masted, gaff-rigged centerboard schooner, the *Quinnipiack* was designed along the lines of a Biloxi, Mississippi, cargo and oyster schooner. These shallow draft schooners carried freight or dredged for shellfish along the Mississippi Gulf coast in the late 1900s.

The *Quinnipiack* was built in Milbridge, Maine, by Capt. Steve Pagels from the design of Howard I. Chappelle and sailed as a charter schooner out of Bar Harbor, Maine. The vessel is noteworthy in that she is almost entirely built from the wood of native Maine "hackmatack," the Algonquian Indian name for a type of North American larch. In 1990 she was purchased by Schooner, Inc., to serve as a platform for environmental education programs. Her design is ideal for the coastal and estuarine studies she pursues.

RARA AVIS

Rara Avis was built similar to a "Thames barge," but instead of its usual spritsails, she was rigged as a three-masted Marconi schooner. She also carries two center-board drop-keels instead of the leeboards associated with barges, which help control stability. She was sold to Father Michel Jaouen and Les Amis de Jeudi-Dimanche Foundation of Paris for 1 franc and now serves as a sail training vessel dedicated to the rehabilitation of young prisoners and drug addicts.

SCANTLINGS
Length overall: 125'
Beam: 23'
Draft: 5' 13"
Hull: Steel
Rig: Marconi schooner
Year built: 1957
Home port: Brest
Flag: France

REGINA MARIS

The "Queen of the Sea," *Regina Maris* was built as a fishing boat in 1908 under the direction of Danish builder J. Ring-Andersen. Brought to the United States in the 1960s, she served on several Arctic explorations for the Ocean Research and Education Society of Boston, Massachusetts. The experience of sailing aboard her during one of her scientific explorations was captured by Harvey Oxenhorn in his book, *Tuning the Rig*, published in 1990.

Since that time, fame, fortune, and financing have not been kind to this once-elegant vessel. Rescued from almost total deterioration and neglect, *Regina Maris* is being brought back to life and sailing condition by Merle Wiggins of the East End Seaport & Marina in Greenport, New York.

SCANTLINGS
Length overall: 144'
Beam: 25'
Draft: 11'
Hull: Wood
Rig: Barkentine
Year built: 1908
Home port:
Greenport, New York
Flag: United States

RETURN OF MARCO POLO

Return of Marco Polo is the English sister ship of the Danish sail training schooner *Den Store Bjørn* in form and function. Almost an exact duplicate in her measurements, *Return of Marco Polo* is also a converted Danish lightship.

Built originally in 1906 for lightship service, *Return of Marco Polo* was retired in 1985. In 1990 she was acquired by the Tvind Organization and converted to her present rigging and function in 1993. She is easily identified by the figurehead of her namesake, the famed Venetian explorer and sailor of the thirteenth and fourteenth centuries.

As does her counterpart, this schooner works with youth and the Tvind Organization and is owned by the Small School at Winestead Hall in Hull, England.

SCANTLINGS
Length overall: 143'
Beam: 22'
Draft: 12'
Hull: Wood
Rig: Schooner
Year built: 1907
Home port: Hull, England
Flag: United Kingdom

ROBERTSON II

A veteran of more than half a century, *Robertson II* has sailed on both great oceans that wash Canada's shores. Built in 1940 of oak, birch, and pine in Nova Scotia, *Robertson II* began her career as a traditional fishing schooner in the Canadian Maritimes and in the Grand Banks fishing grounds. She retired in 1974 and sailed for her new home and career in Victoria, British Columbia, where she serves as part of the Sail and Life Training Society program.

SCANTLINGS
Length overall: 130'
Beam: 22'
Draft: 12'
Hull: Wood
Rig: Schooner
Year built: 1940
Home port: Victoria, British Columbia
Flag: Canada

HMS ROSE

HMS *Rose* is a replica of the British frigate HMS *Rose* built in Hull, England, in 1757. Today's *Rose* was built in 1970 at the Lunenburg shipyard, Nova Scotia, Canada, from original plans in the National Maritime Museum in Greenwich, England. After several ownership transfers, she was acquired by the HMS *Rose* Foundation and extensively rebuilt between 1985 and 1991 to bring her into compliance with Sailing School Vessel and U.S. Coast Guard standards and regulations.

She has a displacement of 500 tons and carries 13,000 square feet of sail. Despite looking like a cover model for a Patrick O'Brian novel, the HMS *Rose* has adapted to the concerns of the present. The same picturesque, billowing sails are technically and environmentally state-of-the-art innovations. They are made of recycled plastic beverage bottles and car fenders. HMS *Rose* has three masts, a flying jib on the bow, a spanker on the stern, and boasts twenty-four cannons.

SCANTLINGS
Length overall: 179'
Beam: 32'
Draft: 13'
Hull: Wood
Rig: Ship
Year built: 1970
Home port: Bridgeport, Connecticut
Flag: United States

SCANTLINGS
Length overall: 137'
Beam: 25'
Draft: 13'
Hull: Wood
Rig: Schooner
Year built: 1925
Home port: Camden, Maine
Flag: United States

ROSEWAY

Until 1975, the *Roseway* was the last pilot schooner still sailing in the United States. She was acquired by the Boston Harbor Pilots' Association in 1941 and served for thirty-four years out of Boston harbor. Originally built as a private fishing vessel in 1925, *Roseway* was built of oak at the J. F. James shipyard in Essex, Massachusetts. In 1975, *Roseway* was refitted for the passenger charter trade of coastal Maine and now has fourteen comfortable cabins. A pine tree, the state tree of Maine, decorates her foremast.

TS ROYALIST

Owned by the Sea Cadets Association of Great Britain, this sail training brig was built in 1971. She carries a permanent crew of eight officers and twenty-four cadets on her sail training cruises.

The Sea Cadets are independent of the royal navy, yet they do receive some navy funding. The aim of the Sea Cadets and the *Royalist* is youth development, but not necessarily to make seafarers of the cadets.

Serious fun is the watchword of the Sea Cadets, who are ages thirteen to eighteen, for whom sailing on the *Royalist* provides both a challenge and adventure. For the Sea Cadets, being on the *Royalist* offers a first real taste of the sea. Each cadet takes part in such watch-keeping duties as steering, lookout, sail handling, and navigation. In turn, each also spends time at more mundane chores, like scrubbing the deck, polishing brass, and peeling potatoes. True to nautical tradition, the Sea Cadets observe the raising of "colors" at sunrise and the lowering of colors at sunset. In addition, most cadets can pipe the ceremonial "Bos'n's Call" to greet returning officers and to announce guests of the ship.

SCANTLINGS
Length overall: 97'
Beam: 19'
Draft: 8' 6"
Hull: Steel
Rig: Brig
Year built: 1971
Home port: Portsmouth, England
Flag: United Kingdom

SAGRES II

Sagres II sails under the Portuguese flag as a naval training ship. She was built in 1937 at the Blohm & Voss shipyard in Hamburg, Germany, and is virtually a sister ship to the *Eagle, Mircea, Tovarishch,* and *Gorch Fock II.* Originally named *Albert Leo Schlageter,* she served under American and Brazilian flags before being acquired by Portugal in 1962. At that time she replaced the first *Sagres,* which was built in 1896 as the *Rickmer Rickmers.* The original *Sagres* has now been restored and serves as a museum ship in Hamburg, Germany.

The name *Sagres* derives from the historic port that sent forth many famed Portuguese explorers and navigators. It served as the home and base for Prince Henry the Navigator (1394–1460). His court in Sagres was responsible for the geographic studies and practical explorations that made Portugal master of the seas in the early fifteenth century. A bust of Prince Henry serves as the figurehead on the bow of *Sagres II,* and the ship is easily identified by the traditional Portuguese crosses of Christ (Maltese crosses) that mark the square sails on her fore- and mainmasts.

SCANTLINGS
Length overall: 293' 6"
Beam: 39' 6"
Draft: 17'
Hull: Steel
Rig: Barque
Year built: 1937
Home port: Lisbon
Flag: Portugal

ST. LAWRENCE

In the early 1950s the Royal Canadian Sea Cadet Corps in Kingston, Ontario, Canada, was a thriving organization in need of a training vessel. When a suitable vessel could not be found, Francis A. MacLachlan, a corps officer and naval architect, designed one: the *St. Lawrence.*

Without government funding, sea cadet officers and other Kingstonians formed Brigantine, Inc., to build and support the vessel. On 5 December 1953, the hull was launched at the Kingston Shipyards. For the next several years cadets and volunteers worked to finish the ship. She was first sailed, unfinished, in 1955 and put into full service as a training ship in 1957. Every summer since then she has sailed as a training ship and now hosts interested youth from the ages of thirteen to eighteen. For the 1986 season she was given a major refit, new machinery, new masts, a new configuration below deck, and a new dedication to train the youth of Ontario.

Her major career highlights include participating in Expo '67 in Montreal; the launching of a sister ship, *Playfair,* by Queen Elizabeth in 1973; an appearance in the U.S. bicentennial celebration in 1976 in New York City; hosting the parade of sail in Kingston in 1984; and representing Canada in 1992 as part of the 250-vessel fleet of the Columbus quincentenary celebration in New York City.

SCANTLINGS
Length overall: 62'
Beam: 13'
Draft: 6' 6"
Hull: Wood
Rig: ~~Barque~~ *Brigantine*
Year built: 1986
Home port: Buffalo, New York
Flag: United States

SCANTLINGS
Length overall: 62'
Beam: 13'
Draft: 6' 6"
Hull: Wood
Rig: Barque
Year built: 1986
Home port: Buffalo, New York
Flag: United States

SEA LION

Sea Lion offers the youth of Buffalo and the Lake Erie region experience aboard a
seventeenth-century barque, recalling the days of early transoceanic adventure.
Built of oak and with hemp used for her standing rigging, *Sea Lion* attempts to be
authentic without sacrificing the safety of her young volunteers and trainees.

135

SEDOV

Sedov is the world's largest tall ship still in service and was one of the last barques built for deepwater cargo carrier service from South America and Australia to the German ports of Bremen and Hamburg. Constructed in 1921 as *Magdalene Vinnen* in Kiel, Germany, she sailed for the Bremen firm of F. A. Vinnen, hence her name. Following the German commercial tradition, she was christened in honor of one of the owner's female family members. After being sold to the shipping conglomerate Norddeutscher Lloyd in 1936, she was renamed *Kommodore Johnson* and served as a sail training vessel. After World War II she was appropriated by the Russian Ministry of Fisheries and was renamed for the Soviet polar explorer and oceanographer Georgij Sedov (1877–1914). *Sedov* is the largest square-rigger still in service from the days of deepwater cargo sailing. She is 10 feet longer than the other giant Russian barque, *Kruzenshtern*.

Besides her physical statistics, such as masts that rise 184 feet above the deck and a length of 386 feet, *Sedov* boasts its own bakery, workshop, and first-aid station. During the tall ship competition of 1992, she also impressed the international fleet with a documented speed of 17 knots in heavy winds. When her thirty-seven sails—covering an area of some 44,000 square feet—fill with a following wind, *Sedov* is a magnificent portrait of sail power.

SCANTLINGS
Length overall: 386'
Beam: 48'
Draft: 27'
Hull: Steel
Rig: Four-masted barque
Year built: 1921
Home port: Murmansk
Flag: Russia

SHABAB OF OMAN

Built in Scotland in 1971 as a sail training vessel, *Shabab of Oman* was acquired by the Sultanate of Oman in 1979. *Shabab of Oman,* which means "youth of Oman," serves as a training ship for the royal navy of Oman and also trains young men from other Omani government bureaus.

The sculptured figurehead on her bow is a replica of the fifteenth-century Omani mariner Ahmed bin Majed, who helped the Portuguese sailor Vasco da Gama explore Africa and India. The turban-clad Majed cuts a rakish figure, wearing a green sash and red "khunjar," a traditional dagger. The red coat-of-arms of the sultanate is recognizable on the sails of *Shabab of Oman* and consists of a khunjar superimposed on a pair of crossed scimitars.

SCANTLINGS
Length overall: 171'
Beam: 28'
Draft: 15'
Hull: Wood
Rig: Barquentine
Year built: 1971
Home port: Muscat
Flag: Sultanate of Oman

SHENANDOAH

A graceful ocean cruiser, *Shenandoah* is at home on all seven seas. She was built on Shooters Island in New York Harbor in 1902 as an American luxury yacht. This distinctive three-masted schooner has had American, Danish, English, French, German, Italian, and, now, Japanese owners. Throughout her transitions, however, *Shenandoah* has remained stately, with long, elegant lines. While she was owned by Baron Marcel Bich she returned to the Atlantic coast of the United States, specifically to Newport, Rhode Island, for the French challenge to the 1974 America's Cup. *Shenandoah* combines an elegant profile with luxurious accommodations and is comfortable in Newport or St. Tropez but best under blue skies, in open water, reaching windward.

SCANTLINGS
Length overall: 163'
Beam: 28' 2"
Draft: 15' 6"
Hull: Steel
Rig: Schooner
Year built: 1902
Home port: Bangkok
Flag: Thailand

SCANTLINGS
Length overall: 142'
Beam: 26'
Draft: 14'
Hull: Wood
Rig: Schooner
Year built: 1942
Home port: Boothbay, Maine
Flag: United States

SHERMAN ZWICKER

One of the last wooden schooners built to fish the Grand Banks off Newfoundland, Canada,
Sherman Zwicker was built in 1942 in Lunenburg, Nova Scotia. Like *Robertson II,* she has adapted
to other duties and now serves the Maine Maritime Museum in Bath, Maine.

SIMON BOLIVAR

Simon Bolivar was one of four barques built in Spain for Latin American countries. Similar in design and rigging, the four ships are nearly identical sister ships: *Gloria* from Columbia, *Guayas* from Ecuador, *Cuauhtemoc* from Mexico, and *Simon Bolivar*. All four are frequent visitors to the United States and at major tall ship gatherings.

The 270-foot *Simon Bolivar* was completed in 1980 and named for the "great liberator" of northern South America. Bolivar (1783–1830) was instrumental in the independence of Columbia, Ecuador, Panama, Peru, and Venezuela.

Simon Bolivar embodies the spirit of idealism and freedom of her namesake. Her figurehead is an allegorical depiction of Liberty and was designed by the Venezuelan artist Manuel Felipe Rincon.

SCANTLINGS
Length overall: 270'
Beam: 35'
Draft: 14' 6"
Hull: Steel
Rig: Barque
Year built: 1980
Home port: La Guaira
Flag: Venezuela

SIR FRANCIS DRAKE

Originally built in 1917 in Luhring, Germany, Sir Francis Drake was refitted as a luxury yacht in 1979–81.
Currently registered in Honduras, this staysail schooner operates as a charter vessel primarily in the Caribbean.
She is owned by Tall Ships Adventures and can accommodate thirty-four passengers on "romantic" Caribbean
sailing adventures. The vessel's name honors Sir Francis Drake (1543–96), who served under Elizabeth I and
whose naval exploits marked him as one of the greatest explorers and privateers of all time.

SCANTLINGS
Length overall: 165'
Beam: 23'
Draft: 9'
Hull: Steel
Rig: Schooner
Year built: 1917
Home port: Tortola,
British Virgin Islands
Flag: Honduras

SIR WINSTON CHURCHILL

The first of two schooners built for England's Sail Training Association, *Sir Winston Churchill* has provided sail training for thousands of young people since 1966. The importance and value of preserving the tradition of tall ships originated with two visionary men, Comdr. Peter Goodwin, Earl Mountebatten, and John Illingsworth. They founded the Sail Training Association, which organized the first small gathering of tall ships in 1956. The success of that first tall ship event generated great enthusiasm for sail training and eventually prompted construction of the STA schooners, *Sir Winston Churchill* and her sister ship, *Malcolm Miller,* in 1968. Designed by noted marine architectural firm Camper & Nicholson, both ships have sailed around the world to participate in tall ship events.

SCANTLINGS
Length overall: 150'
Beam: 26' 8"
Draft: 15'
Hull: Steel
Rig: Topsail schooner
Year built: 1966
Home port: Hull, England
Flag: United Kingdom

SØREN LARSEN

A television star, *Søren Larsen* appeared in the popular BBC series "The Onedin Line" before resuming her more traditional sailing function in the 1st Fleet Reenactment in Australia in 1987 and the Grand Columbus Regatta in 1992, representing New Zealand.

Originally built in Denmark, she was acquired by the Jubilee Sailing Trust in 1983 and has been a part of Square Sail Pacific, which is based in New Zealand, and serves as sail training vessel.

SCANTLINGS
Length overall: 145'
Beam: 25' 6"
Draft: 11' 3"
Hull: Wood
Rig: Brigantine
Year built: 1949
Home port: Auckland, New Zealand
Flag: United Kingdom

SØRLANDET

One of the smallest but more traveled of the full-rigged school ships, *Sørlandet* has had a difficult history since her launch in 1927. Built as a school ship, she was drafted into cargo and transport service and was also used as a storage depot in World War II, when she was heavily damaged. Returned to Norway after the war, she was adopted by the town of Kristiansand, her home port, and has been refurbished for both adventure and educational purposes.

Sørlandet has an exceptional heritage, coming as she does from the days of tall ships and fast clippers. She is now owned and operated by a public foundation, the *Sørlandet* Seilende Skoleskibs Institution, which is controlled and partly funded by the Norwegian Department of Culture. Participation in cruises on *Sørlandet* is open to anyone between the ages of sixteen and seventy-five of either sex and any nationality.

SCANTLINGS
Length overall: 216'
Beam: 29' 6"
Draft: 14' 6"
Hull: Steel
Rig: Full-rigged ship
Year built: 1927
Home port: Kristiansand
Flag: Norway

SOUNDWATERS

This three-masted *sharpie* is a gaff-rigged schooner and the flagship of the environmental organization Soundwaters, which is dedicated to the restoration and preservation of Long Island Sound. Sharpies were first used in the Connecticut oyster fishery industry, and the design spread throughout the eastern seaboard. With very shallow draughts, they were wide-beamed, flat-bottomed, used centerboards, and could be rigged as sloops or schooners.

In addition to sail training, *Soundwaters* sails between ports along Long Island Sound from 15 April to 15 November introducing young people and adults to the ecology of the Sound by reviewing its history and marine science.

SCANTLINGS
Length overall: 80'
Beam: 16'
Draft: 2' 9" (8' 8" lowered centerboard)
Hull: Steel
Rig: Schooner
Year built: 1986
Home port: Stamford, Connecticut
Flag: United States

SPIRIT OF
MASSACHUSETTS

The *Spirit of Massachusetts* is a traditionally rigged, wooden, two-masted schooner based on a nineteenth-century design for a Gloucester fishing vessel, the *Fredonia*. The original design, by Edward Burgess, was drawn in 1889 for a "fast and able" vessel to fish the Grand Banks and Georges Banks of the North Atlantic. Like many New England fishing vessels, *Spirit* incorporates design features that ensure speed and versatility as well as resilience in the face of harsh conditions at sea.

Construction of the schooner began in Boston under the auspices of the New England Historic Seaport in 1983, and *Spirit of Massachusetts* was commissioned in 1984. The design uses a wide variety of timber from many regions of the United States. *Spirit* now supports an extensive sail training and youth program in the waters of the U.S. east coast and the Caribbean. Since her launching, *Spirit of Massachusetts* has traveled more than 100,000 miles and has been seen by millions of people. She is a most unusual educational tool and is open to all.

SCANTLINGS
Length overall: 125'
Beam: 24'
Draft: 10'
Hull: Wood
Rig: Schooner
Year built: 1984
Home port: Boston, Massachusetts
Flag: United States

STAR PILOT

Known as *Pilot* in the northeast waters of the Atlantic, this weathered veteran served for more than fifty years as a pilot boat for the Boston Harbor Pilots' Association. One of the last Gloucester schooners built, her owners hoped to challenge the great Nova Scotian schooner *Bluenose* for the Fisherman's Cup. *Pilot* was purchased by the Association before her completion in 1924. In 1986 she still showed great speed by winning the Esperanto Cup in the annual schooner races off Gloucester, Massachusetts.

In 1994 she sailed more than 7,500 miles from Gloucester to her new home and service as an oceanographic and sail training vessel in San Diego, California. She was rechristened *Star Pilot* and has been recertified by the U.S. Coast Guard for service at the San Diego Maritime Museum.

SCANTLINGS
Length overall: 154'
Beam: 25'
Draft: 14'
Hull: Wood
Rig: Schooner
Year built: 1924
Home port: San Diego, California
Flag: United States

S T A T S R A A D L E H M K U H L

Statsraad Lehmkuhl is Norway's largest and oldest square-rigged sailing ship. She is a three-masted barque built in 1914 at the J. C. Tecklenborgwerft yard in Bremerhaven, Germany, as a training ship for the German merchant navy. Originally christened *Grossherzog Fridrich August,* she saw no service during World War I.

In 1923, she was purchased by agents in Bergen for the Norwegian Shipowners Association on the initiative of secretary of state Kristoffer Lehmkuhl. For his work in promoting the cause of cadet ships and for his contributions to the creation of an independent Norwegian government in 1905, the ship was renamed in his honor.

In 1924 the training ship was transferred to the Bergen Schoolship Association, which operated the vessel through difficult years until 1979 under the direction of Hilmar Reksten.

In 1979, the ship was donated to Stiftelsen Seilskipet Statsraad Lehmkuhl, or the *Statsraad Lehmkuhl* Sailing Vessel Foundation. The board of directors of this foundation comprises representatives of national and local governments, the Maritime Museum of Bergen, the firm of Hilmar Reksten, and the city of Bergen. All are committed to restoring and operating the vessel as a cadet ship. Today she carries young people across oceans to discover the romance of the sea and the adventure of sailing.

SCANTLINGS
Length overall: 321' 6"
Beam: 41'
Draft: 17'
Hull: Steel
Rig: Barque
Year built: 1914
Home port: Bergen
Flag: Norway

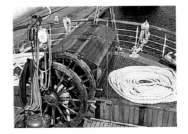

SWAN FAN MAKKUM

Majestic and graceful, *Swan Fan Makkum* is one of the newest tall ships to join the international fleet. An elegant brigantine carrying five square sails on her foremast, *Swan Fan Makkum* offers exceptional accommodations in a true windjammer environment. She is billed as the world's largest brigantine and has an overall length of 203 feet. *Swan Fan Makkum* carries as many as fourteen sails as she sets a course for the Baltic, the North Sea, or, in winter, the Canary Islands and the Caribbean.

SCANTLINGS
Length overall: 203'
Beam: 30'
Draft: 12' 3"
Hull: Steel
Rig: ~~Barkentine~~ *Brigantine*
Year built: 1993
Home port: Makkum
Flag: Netherlands

THOR HEYERDAHL

Named for the Norwegian explorer and anthropologist Thor Heyerdahl, this low-slung topsail schooner is devoted to cross-cultural exchanges and transoceanic scientific expeditions from its land base in Kiel, Germany.

Thor Heyerdahl is remembered for his 1947 reenactment of two voyages across the Pacific in the *Kon-Tiki,* as well as for his 1969 voyage across the Atlantic to the Caribbean in *Ra.* Both voyages sought to prove the possibility of cultural transmigration in primitive seagoing vessels.

SCANTLINGS
Length overall: 164'
Beam: 21' 6"
Draft: 7' 6"
Hull: Iron
Rig: Topsail schooner
Year built: 1930
Home port: Kiel
Flag: Germany

TOLE MOUR

Designed and built in Seattle, Washington, in 1988, *Tole Mour* served as a floating hospital in the Marshall Islands of the South Pacific under the auspices of the Marimed Foundation of Hawaii. The vessel's name was the winning selection from a contest to name the ship held for school children in the Republic of the Marshall Islands. The name means "gift of life and health" in Marshallese.

Tole Mour was chartered by VisionQuest of Pennsylvania to serve as a residential setting and school for adjudicated youth. In 1994 this 156-foot topsail schooner visited various ports on the Great Lakes and the east coast of the United States. *Tole Mour* has now returned to Honolulu, Hawaii, her home port, to continue providing programs for disadvantaged youth in the islands.

Tole Mour was designed by Ewbank, Brooke, and Associates of Auckland, New Zealand, and is nearly a sister ship of the national sail training ship of New Zealand, *Spirit of New Zealand.*

SCANTLINGS
Length overall: 156'
Beam: 31'
Draft: 13' 6"
Hull: Steel
Rig: Topsail schooner
Year built: 1988
Home port: Honolulu
Flag: United States

TOVARISHCH

Originally christened *Gorch Fock, Tovarishch* was the prototype design for the four school ships that were built during the 1930s at the Blohm & Voss shipyard in Hamburg, Germany. Her design was again used for the construction of *Gorch Fock II* in the 1950s.

Tovarishch seems to possess phoenixlike qualities. As *Gorch Fock* she survived World War II only to be scuttled in the waters of the Baltic off Stralsund, a small harbor northeast of Rostock, Germany, in May 1945. For three years she rested in 75 feet of water until she was raised and refurbished by the Soviet Republic. After assignment to the Black Sea for several decades, she began flying the blue-and-yellow flag of Ukraine in 1992.

Tovarishch, or "comrade," usually sets twenty-five sails: ten square sails and fifteen fore-and-aft sails.

SCANTLINGS
Length overall: 263'
Beam: 39' 6"
Draft: 17' 6"
Hull: Steel
Rig: Barque
Year built: 1933
Home port: Khersone
Flag: Ukraine

TREE OF LIFE

Built in Nova Scotia using the latest techniques of a wood-epoxy composite, this gaff-rigged schooner recalls the great schooner building tradition of the Canadian Maritimes. Based in Alexandria, Virginia, *Tree of Life* is a private yacht that sails with a crew of five.

SCANTLINGS
Length overall: 90'
Beam: 19'
Draft: 8'
Hull: Wood and epoxy
Rig: Schooner
Year built: 1991
Home port:
Alexandria, Virginia
Flag: United States

URANIA

Urania is the flagship of the Royal Netherlands Naval College. Every executive officer who has graduated from the naval college over the past forty years trained on *Urania*. Generally she sails with three officers, two petty officers, and twelve cadets. She is a very active ship and has thrice been the recipient of the prestigious Cutty Sark Trophy, which is awarded annually to a ship that best demonstrates the spirit of sail training. Her original wishbone rig was modified to her present Bermudian ketch rig in the late 1950s.

SCANTLINGS
Length overall: 78'
Beam: 18'
Draft: 9' 10"
Hull: Steel
Rig: Ketch
Year built: 1928
Home port: Den Helder
Flag: Netherlands

VICTORY CHIMES

Nearly a century ago *Edwin and Maud* slid down the ways at Bethel, Delaware, and began her remarkable career as a sailing schooner. Built of Georgia pine, live oak *(Quercus Virginia)*, and Delaware oak, she was designed to carry lumber up and down the shallow bays and rivers of the Chesapeake Bay. After serving for more than fifty years, *Edwin and Maud* was purchased by Domino's Pizza, Inc., in 1988 and received a major and much-needed refurbishing. In 1990 she was acquired by her present owners, Capt. Kip Files and Capt. Paul DeGaeta. Renamed *Victory Chimes,* she joined the fleet of "Downeast" windjammers and now serves as a charter vessel operating out of Rockland, Maine.

SCANTLINGS
Length overall: 170'
Beam: 25'
Draft: 18' with centerboard
Hull: Wood
Rig: Schooner
Year built: 1900
Home port: Rockland, Maine
Flag: United States

WESTWARD

Built in 1961 as a private yacht for around-the-world service, *Westward* combines the graceful design of racing yacht with the construction of an oceangoing ship. She is now one of two vessels sponsored by the Sea Education Association (SEA) of Woods Holes, Massachusetts, and has become as familiar in the harbor at Vineyard Haven, Massachusetts. She is also welcome in many of the Caribbean ports she visits on her semester-long educational cruises. Westward serves as part of a program that offers a high school curriculum and postgraduate research courses.

SCANTLINGS
Length overall: 125'
Beam: 22'
Draft: 12' 6"
Hull: Steel
Rig: Schooner
Year built: 1961
Home port: Woods Hole, Massachusetts
Flag: United States

SCANTLINGS
Length overall: 70'
Beam: 14'
Draft: 6'
Hull: Wood
Rig: Gaff schooner
Year built: 1963
Home port: Abaco
Flag: Bahamas

WILLIAM H. ALBURY

Built by the legendary Bahamian boat builder William H. Albury, this vessel and others of its design are now recognized as Bahamian schooners. *William H. Albury* is a familiar sight among the islands and cays of this beautiful country. William Albury built more than three hundred vessels, most on Man o' War Cay; this 70-foot schooner was his last. Operated by Capt. Joseph Maggio, *William H. Albury* offers a series of scuba and sea exploration programs from Marsh Harbour on Great Abaco Island. *William H. Albury* has represented the Bahamas in several international gatherings of tall ships sponsored by Operation Sail.

YOUNG ENDEAVOUR

Given by the United Kingdom to the government and people of Australia in celebration of that country's bicentenary, *Young Endeavour* serves as Australia's national sail training vessel. She was dedicated with the words of Prime Minister Robert Hawke, "This ship—*Young Endeavour*—bears a name imperishably linked with Captain Cook's great voyage of discovery. And the name itself expresses a great deal of our aspirations for our country." For a land surrounded by the sea, this brigantine is a reminder of the country's maritime heritage. *Young Endeavour*'s arrival in Sydney also heralded the start of a new era of sail training in Australia.

Another Australian link of interest to the world of sail training and tall ships is the pioneering spirit of Capt. Alan Villiers, an Australian born in Melbourne in 1903. In 1934, Captain Villiers purchased *Georg Stage,* renamed her *Joseph Conrad,* and logged over 58,000 miles, advocating ocean adventure and the discipline of sail training as educational goals. His ideas inspired and influenced the founders of England's Sail Training Association and, later, the American Sail Training Association.

Young Endeavour sails with a permanent crew of nine from the Royal Australian Navy and hosts a coeducational crew of twenty-four young people. Each year *Young Endeavour* provides hundreds of youngsters with the opportunity to participate in one of twenty ten-day voyages off the Australian coast.

SCANTLINGS
Length overall: 144' 6"
Beam: 25' 6"
Draft: 13'
Hull: Steel
Rig: Brigantine
Year built: 1987
Home port: Sydney
Flag: Australia

SCANTLINGS
Length overall: 141'
Beam: 22' 3"
Draft: 15'
Hull: Steel
Rig: Schooner
Year built: 1952
Home port: Gdansk
Flag: Poland

ZAWISZA CZARNY

This distinctive schooner, with its unusual wishbone rig, is the flagship of the Polish Pathfinders Union, the Polish version of Sea Scouts. *Zawisza Czarny* was named for the legendary hero of the battle of Grunwald in 1404. One of the last great medieval battles in Poland, Grunwald saw Polish knights under the leadership of Wladislav IV defeat an army of Teutonic knights, thus saving eastern Europe from their dominance. This vessel carries a figurehead of her namesake on her bow and a graphic logo on her square-foresail as reminders to young trainees of the ideals of reliability, courage, and duty embodied by *Czarny's* legacy.

Zawisza Czarny has participated in many festivals, races, and gatherings of tall ships and is a favorite with other crews in the ports she visits. She is noted for her hospitable nightly folk music gatherings and sing-alongs.

The present vessel is the second to be named for Czarny. The original *Zawisza Czarny* was a staysail schooner that served until the outbreak of World War II. Owing to deterioration she was scrapped in 1946. In 1952 reconstruction on a fishing trawler—the current *Zawisza Czarny*—was begun at the Stocznia Polnocna shipyard in Gdansk. Major overhauls in 1965, 1968, and 1980 resulted in her present arrangement, which includes a ballasted keel, three steel masts, and an extended stern.

Her unusual rig, with three staysails set in front of the fore-, main-, and mizzenmasts, carries a complement of eleven sails with a total area of 6,000 square feet. In addition to staysails, she carries a square-foresail before the wind as well as a raffe, which is a small, triangular sail that is hung from the top of mast and secured to the yard below.

ZENOBE GRAMME

Serving first as a coastal survey ship, *Zenobe Gramme* is now used as a training ship for the Belgian navy. She is a frequent participant in sail training races and gatherings. Before the wind *Zenobe Gramme* is easily recognized when she sets her spinnaker, which displays the Belgian royal coat-of-arms. *Zenobe Gramme* is named for the Belgian inventor who perfected the technology for alternating-current motors and generators in the 1860s and 1870s.

SCANTLINGS
Length overall: 93'
Beam: 22' 6"
Draft: 8' 6"
Hull: Wood
Rig: Bermuda ketch
Year built: 1961
Home port: Zeebrugge
Flag: Belgium

ZEELANDIA

This three-masted Dutch schooner is notable for her small, curved bow, rounded counter stern, and extremely shallow draft. Requiring little water under her keel makes *Zeelandia* handy on the inland waterways of The Netherlands. Referred to as a "klipper," the term describes *Zeelandia's* function, not rig. Dutch klippers appeared at the turn of the century and were the steel-hulled equivalent of the American coasting schooner. They were maneuverable in shallow waters, but also capable of transporting large and heavy cargo. Rigged first as single-masted sloops with exaggerated booms, klippers later stepped two or three masts. *Zeelandia* was converted from a cargo carrier to her present rig as a sail training schooner.

SCANTLINGS
Length Overall: 128' 6"
Beam: 17'
Draft: 3' 6"
Hull: Steel
Rig: Schooner
Year built: 1931
Homeport: Leeuwarden
Flag: The Netherlands

SCANTLINGS
Length overall: 158'
Beam: 25'
Draft: 16'
Hull: Wood
Rig: Schooner
Year built: 1924
Home port:
Seattle, Washington
Flag: United States

ZODIAC

This elegant schooner was built in 1924 as a private yacht for the family who earned its fortune from the Johnson and Johnson pharmaceutical company. *Zodiac* tested her sails and lines in a transatlantic race from New York to Spain in 1928 and then fell into less lofty service for forty years as a pilot boat for the San Francisco Bay Pilots Association. Delivered from that assignment in 1972 by father and son Karl and Timothy Mehrer, *Zodiac* was the subject of a U.S. Act of Congress in 1982 that placed her on the National Register of Historic Places and ensured her preservation and continued service as a sailing vessel. She now operates out of Seattle and is a familiar sight on Puget Sound.

MARITIME MUSEUMS

AUSTRALIA

Australian National Maritime Museum
Darling Harbor
GPO Box 5131, Sydney
New South Wales 2001

Queensland Maritime Museum
P.O. Box 197
Hamilton
Queensland 4007

South Australian Maritime Museum
135 St. Vincent St.
Post Adelaide
South Australia 5015

Tasmanian Maritime Museum
Secheron House, Battery Point
Hobart 7001

Western Australian Maritime Museum
(home to STS *Leeuwin;* artifacts of *Batavia*)
Old Commiserat Building
Cliff Street
Freemantle 6160

CANADA

Maritime Museum of the Atlantic
1675 Lower Water Street
Halifax, Nova Scotia B3J 153

Maritime Museum of British Columbia
28 Bastion Square
Victoria, British Columbia V8W 1H9

Marine Museum of the Great Lakes
55 Ontario Street
Kingston, Ontario K7L 2Y2

Vancouver Maritime Museum
1905 Ogden Avenue
Vancouver, British Columbia V6J 1A3

FINLAND

Stiftelsen Ålands Sjöfartsmuseum
Hamngaten 2 - PB 98
Mariehamn 22101

GERMANY

Deutschen Schiffahrtsmuseum
(home to *Seute Derne*)
Columbus Center
Bremerhaven

HOLLAND

Scheepvaartmuseum
(home to *Amsterdam* and *Batavia*)
Kattenburgerplein 1
Amsterdam 1018 KK

Holland Glorie
(home to *Europa, Österschelde, Antigua*)
Industrieweg 135
3044 As Rotterdam

UNITED STATES

CALIFORNIA
Nautical Heritage Museum
(home to *Californian*)
24532 Del Prado
Dana Point, California 92629

San Diego Maritime Museum
(home to *Star of India* and *Star Pilot*)
1386 North Harbor Drive
San Diego, California 92101

San Francisco Maritime National Historic Park
(home to *Alma, Balclutha* and *C.A. Thayer*)
2905 Hyde Street
San Francisco, California 94109

CONNECTICUT
The Aquaculture Foundation and Maritime Center
(home to HMS *Rose* and *Black Pearl*)
Captain's Cover
1 Bostwick Avenue
Bridgeport, Connecticut 06605

Mystic Seaport and Museum
(home to *Joseph Conrad, L.A. Dutton,
Charles W. Morgan*)
75 Greenmanville Avenue
Mystic, Connecticut 06355

FLORIDA
Apalachicola Maritime Museum
P.O. Box 625
Apalachicola, Florida 32329

HAWAII
Hawaii Maritime Center
(home to *Falls of Clyde*)
Pier 7
Honolulu, Hawaii 96813

MAINE
Maine Maritime Museum
(home to *Sherman Zwicker*)
243 Washington Street
Bath, Maine 04532

MARYLAND
Chesapeake Bay Maritime Musuem
Navy Point
St. Michael's, Maryland 21663

MASSACHUSETTS
Boston National Historical Park
(home to the USS *Constitution*)
Charlestown Navy Yard
Charlestown, Massachusetts 02129

New England Historic Seaport
(home to *Spirit of Massachusetts*)
Pier 3
Charlestown Navy Yard
Charlestown, Massachusetts 02129

Peabody Essex Musuem
East India Square
Salem, Massachusetts 01970

Salem Maritime National Historic Site
174 Derby Street
Salem, Massachusetts 01970

Sea Education Association
(home to *Corwith Cramer* and *Westward*)
P.O. Box 6
Woods Hole, Massachusetts 02543

MICHIGAN
Michigan Maritime Museum
Dyckman Avenue
South Haven, Michigan 49090

Traverse Tall Ship Company
(home to *Malabar* and *Manitou*)
13390 South West Bay Shore Drive
Traverse City, Michigan 49684

MISSISSIPPI
Maritime and Seafood Industry Museum
(home to *Glenn L. Swetman* and *Mike Sekul*)
P.O. Box 1907
Biloxi, Mississippi 39533

NEW JERSEY
Delaware Bay Schooner Project
P.O. Box 57
Dorchester, New Jersey 08316

NEW YORK
Buffalo Maritime Society
(home to *Sea Lion*)
90 Liberty Terrace
Buffalo, New York 14215

East End Seaport and Marine Foundation
(home to *Regina Maris*)
One Bootleg Alley
Greenport, New York 11944

Hudson River Maritime Center
1 Rondout Landing
Kingston, New York 12401

South Street Seaport
(home to *Wavertree, Peking, Pioneer
and Lettie Howard*)
207 Front Street
New York, NY 10038

NORTH CAROLINA
North Carolina Maritime Museum
315 Front Street
Beaufort, North Carolina 28516

Southport Maritime Museum
116 North Howe Street
Southport, North Carolina 28461

OHIO
Maritime Museum at Put-in-Bay
Put-in-Bay, Ohio 43456

Inland Seas Maritime Musuem
Great Lakes Historical Society
480 Main Street
Vermillion, Ohio 44089

OREGON
Oregon Maritime Center and Musuem
113 Southwest Front Avenue
Portland, Oregon 97204

PENNSYLVANIA
The Flagship *Niagara*
Pennsylvania Historical and Museum
Commission
(home to *Niagara*)
164 East Front Street
Erie, Pennsylvania 16502

Independence Seaport Museum
211 South Columbus Boulevard
Philadelphia, Pennsylvania 19106

RHODE ISLAND
International Yacht Restoration School
(home to *Coronet*)
28 Church Street
Newport, Rhode Island 02640

Museum of Yachting
Fort Adams
P.O. Box 129
Newport, Rhode Island 02840

TEXAS
Texas Seaport Musuem
2016 Strand
Galveston, Texas 77550

VIRGINIA
Nauticus National Maritime Center
One Waterside Drive
Norfolk, Virginia 23510

The Mariners Museum
100 Museum Drive
Newport News, Virginia 23606

WASHINGTON
Gray's Harbor and Historical Seaport
(home to *Lady Washington*)
813 East Heron Street
Aberdeen, Washington 98520

WISCONSIN
Milwaukee Maritime Center
500 North Harbor Drive
Milwaukee, Wisconsin 53202

Wisconsin Maritime Museum
75 Maritime Drive
Manitoc, Wisconsin 54220

GLOSSARY

THIS VERY BRIEF GLOSSARY
DEFINES NAUTICAL TERMS
USED IN THE TEXT.

barque a vessel of three or more masts, all square-rigged except the mast nearest the stern which is fore-and-aft rigged

barquentine a vessel of three or more masts only the foremost of which is square-rigged the others are rigged fore-and-aft

beam the measurement of a vessel at its maximum width

Bermuda sail a tall, triangular, fore-and-aft rigged sail which originated on small boats around Bermuda

bisquine a two-masted fishing boat of traditional French design rigged with lug sails

boom a spar to which the foot of a sail is set

bow the foremost part of a vessel

bowsprit a spar extending over the bow of a vessel to which the foremast is secured by means of a forestay; a jib sail can be set from the forestay

brig a two-masted vessel, both masts rigged with square sails and carrying a fore-and-aft rigged sail on the stern side of the main mast

brigantine a two masted vessel similar to a brig, but omitting the large "course" or square sail on the main mast

capstan a barrel-like device around which a ship's line is wound to lift heavy objects such as an anchor; traditionally powered by crew members pushing on wooden bars

caravel a vessel sailed widely on the Mediterranean by the Portuguese and Spanish between the 14th and 17th centuries; at first lateen-rigged (caravela latina) also rigged with square sails (caravela rotunda); Columbus's *Nina* began her voyage to the Americas as a caravela latina

centerboard a device lowered from the center of a shallow-draught vessel which resists the sideways pressure of the wind and, in doing so, creates forward movement

chine point where the bottom and sides of a vessel meet; when the angle at that point is pronounced the boat is said to have a hard-chine

clipper any one of a number of fast sailing ships; the first vessels so described were Baltimore clippers which were actually rigged as schooners; later designs altered the rig, but in general clippers had hulls deeper aft than forward, sharply raked masts, an overhanging stern, and carried more sail than other ships of comparable size

draught (also draft) measurement between the waterline and the keel; a shallow-draught vessel draws little water

figurehead a carved figure on the bow of a vessel which reflects its name or function

foot bottom edge of a triangular or square sail

fore-and-aft rigged a vessel with sails set parallel to the length of the vessel

full-rigged a ship of at least three masts each fitted with a topmast, top gallant mast, and royal mast, all rigged with yards and square sails

gaff a spar laced to the head of a four-sided, fore-and-aft sail used to hoist and set the sail

gaff-rigged a vessel with four-sided, fore-and-aft sails; the head of each sail is laced to a gaff which extends aft of the mast and parallel to the boom to which the sail's foot is laced

galleass designed originally as warships, these vessels were used during 15th and 16th century naval engagements; armed with a ram, they were powered by both sails and banks of oars; by the 17th century, the galleass had evolved to a three-masted lateen-rigged vessel with one bank of oars

head the top edge of a four-sided sail

hull the body of a vessel

ketch a two-masted fore-and-aft rigged vessel; the second or mizzenmast is shorter than the mainmast and is stepped ahead of the steering position

jib a triangular sail set on a stay or line running from the foremast to the bowsprit or bow; traditional ships carried as many as six jibs

jibe (or gybe) changing the course or direction of a vessel while keeping the wind across the stern

junk name applied to Far Eastern sailing vessels characterized by flat bottoms, square bows, and high sterns rigged with lug sails stiffened horizontally by battens

keel the backbone of a ship's hull to which the stem, stern, and hull framing are attached

knot the nautical measure of speed; one nautical mile equals 6,080 feet

lateen sail a triangular sail set on a yard which raises the sail and then hangs at about a 45 degree angle to the mast; the foot of the sail is not lashed to a boom

leeboard a device lowered from the side of a shallow-draught vessel which resists the sideways pressure of the wind and in doing so creates forward movement

length overall measurement of a vessel from the foremost part of the stem post to the aftermost part of the stern

luff leading or front edge of a fore-and-aft sail

lug sail a four-sided, fore-and-aft sail narrower at its head than its foot which hangs from a lug or gaff which extends both fore and aft of the mast on which it is hoisted

mainmast largest mast on a ship

mainsail a vessel's principal sail; on a square-rigged ship, the bottommost and largest sail on the mainmast

mast a vertical spar from which sails are set

mizzenmast the mast nearest the stern of a vessel with three masts; the aftermast of a ketch or yawl

raffee a triangular sail hung from the stays at the top of a mast to the yard of a square sail below; set in light winds it is also known as a moon-raker

rake the degree of angle away from perpendicular at which a mast is set

rig a vessel's arrangement of masts and sails

schooner a two-masted fore-and-aft rigged vessel with the foremast shorter than the mainmast and originally built in the 1700s at Gloucester, Massachusetts; a familiar variation is the fore-and-aft schooner which carries from two to seven masts all of equal height, rigged fore-and-aft with topsails, although there are many variations

sheer the curve of a vessel's deck from bow to stern

ship-rigged a vessel with three masts, all carrying square sails and a bowsprit

square-rigged vessel which carries sails hung from yards which are "square" or perpendicular to the mast

square sail a four-sided sail which hangs from a yard set "square" or perpendicular to a mast

staysail a sail, usually triangular, set from a stay or line which supports a mast

stem the foremost hull timber, joined to the keel and to which the planking of the hull is fastened to form the bow of the vessel

stern the rear or after end of a vessel

tack changing the course of a vessel by bringing the bow through the wind

tanbark a traditional method of tanning or treating sails and lines made of cotton of flax to protect them against mildew and rot; changes the color of the sail to a medium brown

thonier a ketch-rigged fishing vessel typical of the French province of Brittany

yard a wood or metal spar from which sails are hung; in square-rigged vessels the yard is set perpendicular to the mast and in lateen rigged vessels the yard crosses the mast diagonally

yawl a two-masted fore-and-aft rigged vessel; the second or mizzenmast is shorter than the mainmast and is stepped behind the steering position

BIBLIOGRAPHY

American Sail Training Association.
Directory of Sail Training Programs and Tall Ships.
Newport, RI: ASTA, 1995. Pp.215.

Bishop, Paul.
Tall Ships and the Cutty Sark Races.
Henley: Aidan Ellis, 1994. Pp. 160.

Blackburn, Graham.
*The Illustrated Encyclopedia of Ships, Boats,
Vessels and Other Water-borne Craft.*
Woodstock, New York:
The Overlook Press, 1978.

Bygholm, Henrik and Peter Haagen and
Carl Aage Kirkegaard.
For Fulde Sejl-Skibe omkring et Sail Training Race.
Frederickshavn, Denmark:
Bygholm, 1981. Pp. 111.

Czasnojc, Marek.
Swiat Wielkich Zagli.
Szczecin: GLOB JV, 1991. Pp. 262.

de Kerchove, René.
International Maritime Dictionary.
New York: Van Norstand Reinhold Co.,
1961. Pp. 1018.

Hamilton, John.
Sail Training: The Message of the Tall Ships.
Northamptonshire, England:
Patrick Stephens, 1988. Pp. 232.

Hollins, Holly.
The Tall Ships Are Sailing.
London: David & Charles, 1982. Pp. 192.

Kåhre, Georg.
*The Last Tall Ships: Gustav Erikson and
the Ål and Sailing Fleets 1872-1947.*
New York: Mayflower Books, 1977. Pp. 208.

Liberman, Cy and Pat.
The Mystique of Tall Ships.
Wilmington, DE:
The Middle Atlantic Press, 1986. Pp. 190.

Lund, Kaj.
Sejler I Sigte ! Sail Ho !
Copehagen: Borgen Forlag, 1986. Pp. 216.

Lund, Kaj.
Vinden er vor.
Vol. 4. Tryk: Narayana Books, 1981. Pp. 160.
Vol. 5, 1982. Pp. 160.

SAIL BREMERHAVEN '95.
Bremerhaven:
Tourismus- Förderungsgesellschaft,
1995. Pp. 144.

SAIL HAMBURG '89.
Edited by Kurt Grobecker and Illa Schütte.
Hamburg: Die Barque, 1989. Pp. 112.

Schäuffelen, Otmar.
Die letzen großen Segelschiffe.
Bielefeld: Delius Klasing, 1994. Pp. 388.

Segelschulschiffe.
Norderstedt, Germany:
Verlag Egon Heinemann, 1977. Pp. 90.